Meeting Mental Breakdown Mindfully

Meeting Mental Breakdown Mindfully introduces the Comprehend, Cope and Connect (CCC) approach, developed and evaluated within mental health services, to a wider audience who need to understand mental health issues, whether for themselves or to support others.

The book deconstructs and normalizes mental breakdown, starting from the individual's inner experience, leading to practical ways of helping people out of distress and impaired functioning, towards the realization of their whole potential. It is based on an understanding of connections in the brain founded in cognitive science, which explains how human functioning can easily go astray. CCC provides a compelling rationale for putting mindfulness at the heart of the solution, along with other ways of coping with emotions and changing behaviour. The approach is brought to life through three illustrative case histories, giving a representative and realistic insight into both the experience of the individual and the workings of the system.

Meeting Mental Breakdown Mindfully will help mental health professionals and those in related fields identify more accurately what people in their organization or under their care are going through.

Isabel Clarke is a consultant clinical psychologist with over 25 years' experience as a therapist in the NHS for people with complex problems. Her innovative approach to mental health that side-steps diagnosis is applied widely in Acute Services and is adapted for IAPT and cross-cultural application.

T0384994

Meeting Mental Breakdown Mindfully

How to Help the Comprehend, Cope and Connect Way

Isabel Clarke

Routledge
Taylor & Francis Group

LONDON AND NEW YORK

First published 2022
by Routledge
2 Park Square, Milton Park, Abingdon, Oxon OX14 4RN

and by Routledge
605 Third Avenue, New York, NY 10158

Routledge is an imprint of the Taylor & Francis Group, an informa business

British Library Cataloguing in Publication Data
A catalogue record for this book is available from the British Library

Library of Congress Cataloging-in-Publication Data
A catalog record has been requested for this book

ISBN: 978-0-367-53367-0 (hbk)
ISBN: 978-0-367-53366-3 (pbk)
ISBN: 978-1-003-08161-6 (ebk)

DOI: 9781003081616/9781003081616

Typeset in Bembo
by Taylor & Francis Books

To Chris Clarke. 22.02.1946–16.04.2019.
We continue together in justice work. There is no time in the
Implicational. Death belongs to time. Love does not.

Contents

Figures

Preface

The previous book about Comprehend, Cope and Connect (CCC – the new therapy development covered in this book), *Third Wave CBT Integration for Individuals and Teams* (Clarke & Nicholls 2018), was aimed primarily at Cognitive Behaviour Therapy (CBT) practitioners delivering the model in a service context. However, the approach has applicability beyond these limitations. It contains features that make it relevant in the wide variety of contexts where it is important for people to understand the mental health difficulties of individuals they are working with, or are in some way responsible for; in order to understand their situation in an empathic, non-medical way that leads naturally to the provision of effective help and support. The emphasis of CCC is about working with strengths and potential, and about trusting the individual to take responsibility for their own recovery, with appropriate support. This makes it particularly relevant to counsellors and coaches, whose strength is empathic engagement and capacity for interpersonal reflection and for peer supporters, recovery workers and others who stand alongside. Their skills chime with the CCC emphasis on tuning into felt sense and collaboratively uncovering the factors that impact upon it.

For those working in areas such as student support, chaplaincy and Human Resources, the world of mental health can feel like one they are excluded from by medical language and conceptualisations. At the same time, they desperately need a straightforward lay understanding and means of supporting those they have responsibility for who are experiencing mental distress, in a context where medically delivered treatment can be hard to access and sometimes heavy-handed. More broadly still, the argument of this book is that mental struggle is a natural and expected part of human life. A more accurate and empathic way into unravelling mental breakdown is of relevance beyond these professional fields.

Acknowledgements

Figures 1.1 and 15.1 first appeared in Clarke, I. (2016). *How to Deal with Anger: A 5-step CBT Plan for Managing Anger and Overcoming Frustration*. London: John Murray Learning. They appear here by permission of Hodder & Stoughton Ltd.

Abbreviations

ACT	Acceptance and Commitment Therapy
BABCP	British Association for Behavioural and Cognitive Psychotherapies
BPS	British Psychological Society
CAT	Cognitive Analytic Therapy
CBT	Cognitive Behaviour Therapy
CCC	Comprehend, Cope and Connect
CEO	Chief Executive Officer
CFT	Compassion Focused Therapy
CMHT	Community Mental Health Team
DBT	Dialectical Behaviour Therapy
DCP	Division of Clinical Psychology
EBE	Experts by experience
ECT	Electro-Convulsive Therapy
EFFA	Emotion Focused Formulation Approach
EUPD	Emotionally Unstable Personality Disorder
IAPT	Increasing Access to Psychological Therapies
ICS	Interacting Cognitive Subsystems
ISP	Intensive Support Programme
MDT	Multi-Disciplinary Team
MHCS	Mental Health Confidence Scale
MBCT	Mindfulness Based Cognitive Therapy
MBT	Mentalization-Based Treatment
NATs	Negative Automatic Thoughts
NICE	National Institute for Clinical Excellence
OT	Occupational Therapy/Therapist
PIP	Personal Independence Payment
PTMF	Power, Threat, Meaning Framework
PTSD	Post-Traumatic Stress Disorder
SAMS	Situationally accessible memory
VAMS	Verbally accessible memory

Section I

Foundations

DOI: 10.4324/9781003081616-1

1 Being human and why it is difficult – a rethink

Introductory summary

The themes of the book will be illustrated by three composite case examples, and these individuals are introduced first; initially as they present and cause concern to others. To lay the foundations for a new approach to the mental health struggles illustrated by these cases, some fundamental assumptions behind the current ortho-doxy are challenged. In order to understand how easy it is for things to go wrong for human beings we need to factor in how our very organ of understanding, our brain, takes short cuts and glosses over discontinuities. The way in which human beings can easily become ensnared between the very different, logical and emotional, ways of knowing is explained, using the Interacting Cognitive Subsystems (ICS) model of cognitive architecture, which provides the scientific basis for CCC. ICS clarifies the central role of felt sense and the way in which past trauma can complicate our internal state, leading to the importance of mindfulness as a means to rebalance and come back to the present. This discussion introduces the alternative, CCC, model of mental health breakdown, which is based on the potential threats to our internal stability inherent in our mental make-up, and how people cope with them.

Being human and why it is difficult – a rethink

Struggle with emotions and relationships is not the exception – it is the rule (what would literature, soap operas etc. be like if it were not?). It is also not that uncommon for such struggles to overwhelm normal coping; to lead to difficulties with keeping up the routines of normal life, or to lead to ways of coping that clearly are not normal, including departures from shared reality. Sometimes it is the individual who is struggling who asks for help in such cases, but often it is those around them who become concerned: employers, family members or others who can see that things are not right. Before launching into the argument of the book, I will introduce the examples of three individuals whose mental struggles are causing concern to others. Their stories and progress will be revisited to illustrate the approach presented throughout the book. These case examples take elements from many people I have worked with over a long therapy career, but without being based on any one person. (I used the cases of real people I treated, who read,

DOI: 10.4324/9781003081616-2

approved and sometimes helped to write the accounts, in my previous book: *A Third Wave CBT Integration for Individuals and Teams: Comprehend, Cope and Connect*, Clarke & Nicholls 2018.) So, let us meet Kath, Tasha and Raju.

Kath, age 35, is causing concern to her employer, an employment agency call centre with tight targets. Kath has worked there for five years – unusual in a high turnover environment. She has an effective phone manner, so performs steadily, while being less aggressive at pursuing targets than some of her colleagues.

Kath is a single parent. Over the years, she has taken about two weeks off each year for depression and is on medication. This year, the depression has dragged on. Three weeks; return to work for a week; a week off; another unsuccessful return; two weeks off. Additionally, there has been friction between the new manager, Cheryl, brought in to sharpen performance, and Kath, who has uncharacteristically lost her temper with Cheryl, then burst into tears and walked out. This was followed by the latest period off work. She keeps wanting to come back to work, sooner than the GP recommends, but then cannot cope. Management are at a loss.

Tasha, age 20, came to the attention of the student support service at the Further Education College she attends. Tasha has been failing to keep up with the work, and has an ongoing problem with self-harm. She clearly has ability, and had been encouraged to study for more ambitious qualifications than the entry course in care work she was currently pursuing, but her complicated family situation and mental health issues seem to limit her horizons. The college is aware of the situation, and of both her extensive history of contact with mental health services, currently the Community Mental Health Team (CMHT), and that of other members of her family. Recently, the self-harm has escalated and become more dangerous, leading to a couple of visits to A&E.

Raju, 30, was causing concern to his wife. Ambika and Raju are a young Asian professional couple. Ambika was making rapid headway in her career in medicine. She had impressed her superiors in her senior hospital post and was ready to embark on challenging exams to become a consultant. This would enable the realization of the couple's dream of selling their flat, buying a house with a garden and starting a family. Expectations from their wider families about children had been mounting in urgency for some time.

However, Raju's career as an accountant had not been progressing well. Recently, he had been getting into arguments with his employers, changing jobs frequently and currently was finding it hard to get another position. He was spending a lot of time at the computer. He had become more withdrawn, but when Ambika pressed him about what he found so absorbing, his response was disturbing. He talked about having followed esoteric courses and gained secret knowledge that would give him a position of power and wealth in the world. He then attributed his problems with employers and job finding to a conspiracy against him, masterminded by enemies of the esoteric sect. When Ambika attempted to express scepticism, he got angry with her. It was when he nearly hit her that she tried to insist he see their GP.

All three of these individuals present with what would be recognized as mental health issues, but in markedly different ways. All have caused concern among interested others because their everyday functioning is in some way affected. Outside pressures can be inferred for each of them: a new manager for Kath, pressure of college work and family for Tasha, and the contrast between his and his wife's career success for Raju. As yet, we do not know what is going on for these individuals themselves.

The central aim of this book is effective help and understanding for people experiencing mental health difficulties such as those illustrated above. What if the way that such difficulties are currently viewed is a major obstacle in achieving this end? This contention requires starting from a different place, and tackling the assumptions that underpin the dominant narrative concerning mental health – a bit like clearing the room and stripping off the old wallpaper before you can create a new decorative scheme.

How we know about the world: assumptions and limitations

Philosophers (like Kant) have always been aware that the world we take for granted is to a greater or lesser extent a construction; a function of our organs of perception and their limitations. The workings of the brain and its interconnections with the sense organs and our body's arousal system all impose limitations and constraints on how we experience and react to the world around us, yet human beings are some-how designed to factor this information out. Consider the way our visual neural apparatus works, as this is relatively simple and there have been extensive experiments (often based on doing unpleasant things to cats) to tease out exactly what is going on. This research concludes that, rather than photographing exactly what is out there, our brains look for features, edges, discontinuities and recognizable shapes, and construct a plausible picture out of this information (e.g. Murray et al. 2002, Luck et al. 1997). Ambiguous pictures illustrate this point; the two faces in profile that can equally appear to be a vase, or the alternating duck and rabbit outline. Choice where to direct attention also affects perception in sometimes surprising ways, as illustrated by the experiment where the instruction to count ball catches while watching a video of a game results in observers failing to note a man in a gorilla costume walking across the pitch (Chabris & Simons 2010).

This feature of human information processing applies much more widely, and, as with the operation of the visual system, it normally goes unnoticed. We work on the assumption that what we see is what is out there. However, we need to recognize that, whenever the brain comes up with something it cannot quite work out, it will present you with a best guess, as if that is 'reality', without any qualification, and that, in addition, what you are looking for affects what you see. This becomes significant when we put it together with the challenging model of the way the brain is wired up that lies at the heart of the CCC approach; the ICS (Teasdale & Barnard 1993) model of cognitive architecture, which will be introduced in more detail in the section that follows.

ICS leads to the realization that we have two separate ways of knowing that give us different but complementary information. We are blissfully unaware of this gap between the two ways of knowing because our brains are designed to smooth over discontinuities and come up with a 'solution' if the data doesn't quite work. However, it is precisely this crack that points to why being human is so difficult, and why our three case examples might be struggling. Another aspect to be explored later suggests the human being is not a closed system as generally assumed, leading to creative potential for connection, communication and healing that can get overlooked. Leonard Cohen refers to the crack where the light gets in.

The claim that there are two distinct ways of knowing is not unfamiliar. A distinction between conceptual and intuitive modes of cognition have long been accepted. The effects of different levels of neural processing in the brain are familiar in everyday life. It is only necessary to consider the difference between normal, calm problem solving and the panic reaction when, for instance, the toddler you had responsibility for has suddenly vanished in a busy mall. Therapy modalities recognize that human reactions become problematic and things go wrong when that panicky, emotion driven mode of processing takes over, and there are a number of ways in which they approach this, some of which will be discussed in Chapter 3. Similarly, there are a number of dichotomous processing theories around in the more general literature, e.g. *Thinking Fast and Slow* (Kahneman 2012) and *The Master and his Emissary* (McGilchrist 2009). I argue that ICS represents a significant advance on these others because:

- It is based on an impressive corpus of experimental data on cognitive processing, coding and limitations.
- It is even-handed. It avoids the trap of favouring one side over the other or assigning dominance. McGilchrist's claim that the left brain has usurped power rightfully belonging to the right brain is an example of this fallacy.
- Above all, it claims that as individuals we have no overall control over the process of exchange between the two systems – as Teasdale and Barnard put it, 'there is no executive function' (Teasdale & Barnard 1993, p. 63 and p. 78). In other words, there is no boss.
- It is this very lack of overall control that opens the way to a completely different perspective on the human being; one that makes vulnerability to breakdown all too comprehensible, along with the search for a satisfactory sense of self.
- I also like it because, properly understood, it should be deeply unsettling.

ICS will be examined in more detail in Chapter 4. We will now consider the way in which the insights offered by the model can illuminate both the human condition in its vulnerability, and how to approach the breakdown that will sometimes inevitably happen.

Essential features of ICS

The diagram in Figure 1.1 gives us the essential ICS at a glance. It is adapted from Dialectical Behaviour Therapy (DBT) and uses DBT terminology, which I will follow for now. ICS terminology will be introduced later.

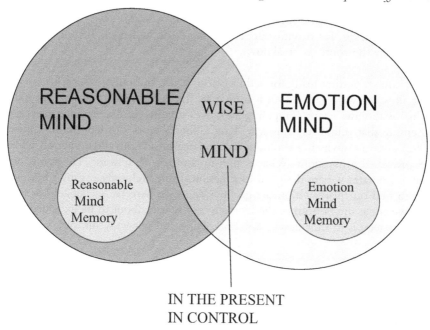

Figure 1.1 Different Circuits in the Brain (Adapted from DBT)

- The two circles represent our two central meaning making systems. They are different in character, because the Emotion Mind connects with the senses and the body's arousal system; Reasonable Mind only connects with our verbal systems.
- They work together most of the time – hence the overlap at Wise Mind.
- But they separate out at high and at low arousal.
- Because their memories (added to the original DBT diagram) are now separate when this happens (and very different in character), the Emotion Mind memory no longer has access to information about context and time.
- In this way, at times of stress, vivid memory of past events can be re-triggered; they might even be re-experienced as present (cf. flashbacks).
- Because Emotion Mind connects with the body's arousal system, this can take over when Emotion Mind is in charge, and it is easy for a vicious cycle to get set up where threat is perceived, the body gets ready for action, the mind is directed to look out for threat, which again signals the body to increased arousal.
- Where there is no action and no cause for action (as is usually the case with the sorts of threats experienced in our society – a traffic jam making us late for something important; an unwelcome email), this causes build-up of stress; panic or loss of temper.

- In simpler societies, these connections made us safe – we got out of the way quickly, faced with our second sabre toothed tiger. In our society it can be the route to breakdown.

Of course, getting ready for action (stress) is not the only reaction to a sense that all is not well. Depression is caused by the body shutting down; the individual withdraws, stops competing and gives themselves discouraging messages to ensure that things stay this way. Paul Gilbert's work on depression (Gilbert 1992) gives a convincing evolutionary explanation for this phenomenon when he answers the question: 'What is the function of depression?' He points out that as primates we are designed to function in hierarchically organized groups and to find our place within the group. When we perceive (accurately or not) that we are at the bottom of the hierarchy, or worse, about to be excluded, the safest strategy is to shut down, stop competing and generally opt out.

Felt sense

The previous paragraphs have described what happens when Emotion Mind is dominant and Reasonable Mind is relatively inaccessible. Where things are considered in Reasonable Mind, they are brought into the light of day – of full consciousness. Where Emotion Mind and the body's arousal system take charge, we are much less fully aware of what is going on. The great breakthrough of psychoanalysis was revealing the hold that 'the unconscious' or 'subconscious' has over our minds. What has been described above is a bit simpler and less mysterious. Human beings are designed for survival in an environment that can deliver both physical and social threats. Survival is priority number one, so that when threat to either is picked up, Emotion Mind and the body essentially take over. This hits our consciousness in the form of gut feeling, of felt sense.

Felt sense is another of those absolutely fundamental aspects of our lives that is simply assumed, so that its power operates unexamined. Emotion Mind is constantly on the lookout for information about safety and social position as part of its role to keep us safe. Research has shown that we constantly monitor the non-verbal behaviour of others to check on this (Decety & Jackson 2004). This translates into: 'What is it like to be me, now?' How we feel inside. This is crucial.

Our society, and all human societies, have prioritized things that modify how we feel inside – from tea, coffee and music to mind altering substances and rituals. More on all that later. Where all is predictable, there is nothing to notice. We experience change, especially for the worse in the gut (e.g. a sudden sense that you have got something wrong in a social situation and the atmosphere has turned frosty). The complicating factor is that, once Emotion Mind is fully in charge, we have lost touch with time, which is managed by Reasonable Mind, and the Emotion Mind memory adds past threat to whatever is going on in the present. This has the potential to render our felt sense unbearable. Where we find something that helps with the unbearable feeling, it can quickly become a rigid pattern that is hard to escape – because when you let go of that immediately useful but ultimately harmful strategy, the unbearable feeling still needs to be faced: and it will be worse than before because avoidance gives what is avoided more power. As we will see, this trap provides a simple way into understanding 'symptoms' of 'mental illness' – they can all be traced to things that help people cope with how they feel inside.

The role of mindfulness

The preceding discussion focuses on the way in which so much that is important for us goes on beneath the surface, beyond our level of awareness. It intrudes into that awareness as our bodies are recruited to take over and we experience that as disruption to our felt sense. Clearly, some means of discerning what is going on and being able to intervene and alter its course is required. This is where the core skill of mindfulness comes in. More will be said about the history of mindfulness as applied to therapy in Chapter 3, but for now it is sufficient to say that mindfulness is simply the practice of becoming` aware of all the information available to the senses, and of the mind's immediate reaction to it. To do this, it is necessary to temporarily disengage from the mental chatter of the mind and refocus onto the body and the surroundings. This is a simple but powerful adjustment of con-sciousness, and it is the beginning of being able to take charge of the situation. Though straightforward, it is not easy to sustain as it runs counter to the normal operation of the thinking mind, which constantly darts between past and future, whereas mindfulness requires staying in the present. In its normal mode of opera-tion, the mind sorts things out into interesting or boring, good or bad, while mindfulness entails letting go of judgements. All this is simple, but difficult.

Return to Kath, Tasha and Raju

If we are to understand Kath, Tasha and Raju better, how they are feeling inside could be important. At the moment, the information is still a bit sparse. Kath has uncharacteristically lost her temper and then displayed distress at work. She has also frequently been feeling too down to come to work. Tasha's habitual self-harm, presumably something she has learnt is helpful in dealing with how she feels inside, has become more severe, suggesting that her internal state has taken a turn for the worse. We have less direct information about what is going on for Raju. How-ever, it cannot feel good to have your career going nowhere while your wife's is taking off, to say nothing of pressure from the wider family. As yet, we do not have information about whether the past is getting mixed up with the present for any of them, but that is likely to be an ingredient in the mix.

Conclusion and summary

In this chapter, we have met Kath, Tasha and Raju, the characters who will translate into real life the themes of the book. The chapter has introduced the theory behind the challenge to conventional thinking about mental health breakdown. It has laid out the bare bones of ICS: the two ways in which the mind operates, the emotional and the logical, along with their intrinsic difference and the lack of any stable, overall, control. This theme will be returned to in more depth in Chapter 4. The role of trauma in breakdown has been indicated. Further exploration of this will occur in Chapter 5. The importance of felt sense and its central role in the model has been explained and the role of mindfulness as a way to rebalance and find a new way forward where things have gone astray has been introduced. We are now ready to explore in more depth what is wrong with the illness model of mental breakdown which this chapter has called into question. However, if these more general issues are of less interest to you, you can skip to Part III, where the practical, 'How to help', section begins – though do follow our three case examples through the intervening sections, identifiable by the headings.

2 Why the conventional wisdom about mental health needs challenging

Introductory summary

This chapter examines the way in which the 'illness' model of mental health has become enshrined within services. The flawed history of the diagnostic manuals and disregard for social and environmental factors in mental breakdown have ensured that, too often, people's stories are not heard and medication is offered as the only solution to their distress. Evidence for the true impact of trauma on development and later difficulties is introduced, along with the limitations of medication. The medical model is held responsible for masking the common vulnerability of human beings, leading to the damaging stigma associated with diagnosis; more with some diagnoses than others. Though therapy has now become more recognized as a core treatment for mental health difficulties, with the introduction of Increasing Access to Psychological Therapies (IAPT) in England, this therapy is most commonly linked to diagnosis. The chapter ends with the current challenges to the diagnostic system by considering the 'Power, Threat, Meaning' Framework (PTMF).

Kath, Tasha, Raju and the mental health system

Chapter 1 laid the foundation for a way of approaching mental health problems that sees them in terms of how people cope with what they are feeling inside. It introduced a model of the way that the brain is wired up that helps to explain the centrality of that 'felt sense' for our perception of safety and danger, and of our sense of who we are in relation to those around us. These factors are central precisely because 'who we are' is not a given, but a dynamically shifting system. The self is process. Much of the time, this underlying dynamic is beyond the reach of conscious awareness, because everything remains roughly the same. We perceive a sense of unease; a gut feeling in the body, when change for the worse threatens – and excitement/exhilaration when change is for the better. This constant, background, balancing act can easily be upset, and the role of the emotional memory, which stores memory for threat across time and presents it when current threat intrudes, can play a powerful role in upsetting this balance.

To return to Kath, Tasha and Raju, they have all been causing concern to those around them; Kath's employers, Tasha's course and Raju's wife. The

DOI: 10.4324/9781003081616-3

mental health services are either involved (Kath and Tasha) or likely to be soon (Raju). In making sense of their predicament, those services are unlikely to see the situation in terms of how they have been managing their internal state and the factors impinging on that state.

Kath has received a diagnosis of recurrent, chronic depression, and has been taking medication to help control this for a long time. Her current difficulties will therefore be categorized as a serious relapse in this condition.

Tasha's difficulties have already been labelled as 'Borderline Personality Disorder' (BPD, also known as Emotionally Unstable Personality Disorder, EUPD). She has presented various challenges to children's and then adult services over the years, and self-harm and periodic suicidality have helped to secure this deeply discouraging diagnosis. It has not as yet led to any straightforward treatment solution. Neither counselling nor the various medications tried have had much impact.

The sharp fear in Ambika's mind as she listens to Raju is that he has 'developed' schizophrenia or some other psychosis diagnosis, meaning that their future looks bleak in the extreme.

The diagnostic view illustrated here represents the most widely available response to mental health difficulties. This approach gives a sense of clarity. It directs clinicians to particular medication and therapy recommendations. Tasha sees the advantage of a BPD diagnosis in terms of securing benefits, while feeling personally insulted by it. The main problems with the diagnostic approach are summarized next.

Objections to diagnosis

- It can obscure what is really going on, particularly with respect to trauma.
- It is unscientific. Psychiatric diagnoses do not identify discrete categories and have no physical basis that can be tested for.
- Research and treatment become shackled to relatively meaningless distinctions, which holds back progress.
- It leads to, or is led by, medical dominance, which has meant an over reliance on drugs, Electro-Convulsive Therapy (ECT) and restriction (e.g. sectioning, observation etc.) as treatment.
- It sets up an 'us and them' dynamic, which masks the inherent instability of the human condition and obscures the fact that mental health 'symptoms' are almost all common behaviours, but engaged in in a way that impacts functioning.

The weight of these objections has gathered strength, and it was probably anticipation of DSM (Diagnostic and Statistical Manual) 5 around 2012 that led to concerted initiatives to question the whole basis of diagnosis by the Critical Psychiatry Network (Bracken et al. 2012), followed by the Division of Clinical Psychology (2013), which has led to the PTMF initiative (www.bps.org.uk/power-threat-meaning-framework, Johnstone & Boyle 2018).

These objections will now be examined along with the evidence.

'What happened to you?'

Diagnosis explains nothing. Worse, it purports to give an explanation, which shuts off enquiry from exploring what is really going on. The movement currently staging the most vigorous assault on the diagnostic approach (Johnstone & Boyle 2018) complains that the core question should be not 'What is wrong with you?' but rather 'What happened to you?' In other words, the adverse life events and trauma that are commonly a major factor in mental health breakdown, because the emotional memory works across time, are disguised and side-lined by viewing diagnosis as sufficient explanation.

There is a growing body of evidence, across the major diagnoses, that trauma and/or earlier adversity is present and almost certainly a causal factor in later breakdown (e.g. Carr et al. 2013; Read & Bentall 2012; Read et al. 2005). As suggested above, mental health research is mostly linked to diagnosis, so I will cover first the case with respect to so-called 'personality disorder' and then psychosis.

Evidence for trauma: so-called 'personality disorder'

It is recognized that people with diagnoses of both antisocial personality disorder and BPD frequently, although not always, have early histories of neglect, violence, abuse and trauma (NIMHE 2003; Herman 2001; van der Kolk 2014.) Bessel van der Kolk and colleagues initiated a concerted and well researched, but unsuccessful, drive to change the designation, particularly of BPD, to 'complex trauma', in DSM IV (more on DSM below). Their research tracked effects of stress on development, in such a way as to demonstrate how early and ongoing adversity can accumulate and produce the characteristic developmental distortions. These distortions essentially arise out of how people understandably manage long term stress effects and the feelings this produces. The title of van der Kolk's 2014 book, *The Body Keeps the Score*, succinctly sums up the way that early and persistent release of stress hormones, in response to experiencing extreme threat, lays the foundation for lifelong hypersensitivity to stress.

A tendency to rely on ways of coping, such as self-harm and substance abuse, that interfere with life functioning can follow from this. This understanding importantly incorporates what we now know about trauma memory, and the way in which such memories are preserved and re-presented, outside of time and context, when triggered in the present. This feature of trauma memory is an important factor in the maintenance of high levels of stress and distress long after the initial stressor has passed, and explains the long term impact of trauma and adversity (van der Kolk 2014, 2008, Masson et al. 2013).

Attachment (Bowlby 1969, 1988, Ainsworth et al. 1978) is another relevant and well researched concept. This underpins the Mentalization approach of Bateman & Fonagy (2004). Attachment explains the strong element of relationship difficulties and avoidance that is evident in all the so-called personality disorder categories. It has relevance as it traces the mapping of an immediate, physically experienced sense of threat, based on early adverse experience, which can persist throughout life and distort patterns of relating. The horrible feeling at the heart of

CCC can be traced back to the desperation of the infant faced with inadequacy in the caring on which his/her life literally depends, in the absence of any other way of getting its needs met. This infant remains, buried deep within the adult, presenting with the sort of difficulties that attract the personality disorder label. Researchers from Schore (1994) onwards have tracked how such early experience impacts the development of the individual's biological stress management capacity, work which underpins the findings of van der Kolk (2014), referred to above.

Trauma and psychosis

As researchers started to ask the questions and make the links, the connection between earlier trauma and childhood adversity and every manifestation of mental health problems became inescapable. Confirming the link for psychosis (Varese et al. 2012 is a widely cited authority) presents the strongest challenge to the idea that 'schizophrenia' is purely biological; an illness with only a strong genetic link for origin. A recent study in fact suggests that the link to trauma is stronger as compared with other diagnoses (Morkved et al. 2017). There are powerful testimonies from experts by experience relating the connection between voices and beliefs and the traumatic events of their earlier life that add weight to this now indisputable connection (e.g. Longden 2013, Dillon 2009).

Diagnosis is unscientific

Dissatisfaction with the prevailing paradigm goes back to Laing (1965, 1967) and Szasz (1974), but Mary Boyle (2002) probably started the systematic attack on the diagnosis of schizophrenia, which has been enthusiastically followed up, with an overwhelming weight of evidence, and then broadened to take in other diagnoses by Richard Bentall (2003, 2009). The story of the evolution of the diagnostic manuals (*Diagnostic and Statistical Manual*, US based, DSM and Classification of Diseases and Related Health Problems, World Health Organization, ICD), which underpin the whole system, is a history of crashing about in the dark. A psychodynamic explanation for mental health difficulties was first adopted by DSM, then abandoned in favour of a physical explanation. The problem was that relics of the earlier conceptualization still hang around (the label 'BPD' is one example of this) and worse, no evidence for a physical basis for any of the main diagnoses has been found, despite extensive and expensive research effort. Seeing mental health as analogous to physical health is thus exposed as illusory.

The diagnostic system depends crucially on there being an array of distinct conditions that can be reliably distinguished by trained clinicians. Nothing could be further from the data. 'Comorbidity' abounds; anyone who has been around the system for any length of time will have acquired an array of diagnoses across the spectrum, as a glance at their notes will confirm. Bentall (2003) has done a thorough job of unmasking this particular fallacy.

This division into separate diagnostic groupings lends rigidity to attempts to specify and evaluate treatment. Traditionally, the first line of treatment has been medication. Latterly, for instance with the introduction of IAPT in England, talking therapy has been given more prominence. Those therapies that have been studied with Randomized Controlled Trials (RCTs) are the gold standard. But such trials rely on diagnostic categories to identify cohorts to study. The (many) people whose problems do not fit neatly into the categories are therefore left out, but the diagnostic system is enshrined even within therapy.

Medication as the main treatment

It is precisely because the diagnostic system positions mental health problems firmly within the medical sphere that medication is seen as the first treatment of choice. Also, medical practitioners, whether GPs or psychiatrists, are much more numerous and so available than therapists and psychologists. Prescribing is quicker and simpler than offering an extended course of therapy, and so cheaper. However, problems with psychotropic medication, of dependence and diminishing returns, as well as side effect issues, have increasingly emerged, and more recently, the fundamental research on which the claims for this medication rest has been called into question (Whitaker 2010, Moncrieff 2008, 2010).

Whitaker argues that these medicines have been oversold, by exposing the flaws in the research on which the claims made for them are based. This research has been predominantly carried out by pharmaceutical companies who have underreported data that throws doubt on the efficacy and safety of their products. In particular, withdrawal problems and longer term morbidity have been swept under the carpet. Moncrieff shows how these medicines have been mis-sold as a cure for fictional illnesses, whereas they actually act in a generic manner on factors like state of arousal. She reveals the circular argument whereby the fact that, for instance, neuroleptics reduce auditory hallucinations is used to 'prove' the existence of schizophrenia as a distinct condition.

The wealth that the pharmaceutical companies can plough into research and publicity means that research into talking therapies lags far behind, and this is reflected in the treatment recommendations in the NICE guidelines. These recommendations decide what treatments can be offered by the British NHS, dependent on research outcomes. Recently there has been some effort to allow therapies to catch up, but still largely tied to diagnostic categories.

Common humanity and the scourge of stigma

All these factors serve to entrench the notion of 'mental illness', both in the health services and, through the media, in the popular imagination. There is much hand wringing about the prevalence of stigma around 'mental illness', but less awareness of the research that shows that this is associated with medical as opposed to social (i.e. life event and life circumstances) understandings of its origins (Read, Haslam & Magliano 2013, Read 2007). Receiving a stigmatizing diagnosis such as 'paranoid schizophrenia' understandably demolishes someone's self-image and vision of their future. Because of the precarious nature of the sense of self, alluded to above, this is a major mental health own goal.

Above all a medical conceptualization of mental health challenges sets up an 'us and them'. It carries within it the assumption that some people are ill, whereas the rest of us are 'well'. This is challenged by the view of the human being as constantly managing a balancing act to secure a good enough sense of self, which can be upset at any time, as there is no boss; the view put forward in Chapter 1. People who find themselves needing to use mental health services are increasingly objecting that they are not a different species, but human beings along with the people who provide treatment; we all struggle at times and are affected by our environment and the things that happen to us. It is just that this struggle overwhelms some people sometimes, and they need support to get back on track. The way that trauma memory operates, and individual differences in temperament and reactivity, based on individual biological difference, but not on 'illness', can make this struggle less easy to manage for some than for others.

The Power Threat Meaning Framework (PTMF)

In response to the sort of criticisms of diagnosis listed above, and following on from the Division of Clinical Psychology (DCP) of the British Psychological Society (BPS)'s document calling for an alternative classification system (DCP 2013), Lucy Johnstone, Mary Boyle and others worked on just such an alternative: the PTMF.

In summary, this framework for the origins and maintenance of distress replaces the question at the heart of medicalization, 'What is wrong with you?' with four others:

- 'What has happened to you?' (How has **Power** operated in your life?)
- 'How did it affect you?' (What kind of **Threats** does this pose?)
- 'What sense did you make of it?' (What is the **Meaning** of these situations and experiences to you?)
- 'What did you have to do to survive?' (What kinds of **Threat Response** are you using?)

The PTMF has developed an initial set of overlapping meta-narratives based on analysis of the core themes in people's personal stories. This is not the central concern of CCC, which is primarily focused on laying bare the mechanism whereby distress originates and is perpetuated, along with a simple enough way of working out what has caused what for each individual, that almost anyone can follow the logic, given the right support. However, the PTMF and CCC can be seen as complementary – the former taking a broader perspective and making explicit links to wider aspects such as social injustice and inequality, and the latter looking at how these patterns may play out in individual lives, and the acute services whose job is to provide interventions in the case of breakdown. The application of CCC in acute services is referred to in PTMF.

Conclusion and summary

This chapter has exposed the scientific flaws in the medical conceptualization of mental health difficulties, along with the damage that the dominance of this model perpetuates. It places CCC in the context of a movement to displace the illness model from its current pedestal and reclaim the social and environmental context behind human struggles. In so doing, it is reclaiming people's stories and attacking the scourge of stigma. Until recently, medication has been the first remedy offered to anyone presenting to their doctor with mental health difficulties, but over the last decade, the central role that therapy can play has at last been recognized and it has been made more accessible; however, this is often therapy cradled within the medical embrace, with specific protocols linked to particular diagnoses. The next chapter will pick up and expand on the current state of therapy provision in the UK, setting CCC in context in relation to the other available therapies.

3 Turning therapy inside out

Introductory summary

This chapter reviews the approaches of different therapy modalities to helping people with mental health difficulties. All modalities seek to understand the operation of the human mind as a whole, not just where there is mental breakdown, in contrast to the medical model covered in the previous chapter. The chapter reviews the history of therapy through the 20th into the 21st century, thus setting the context for the current relative dominance of CBT in the UK. This leads onto consideration of the Third Wave cognitive therapies that are the true home of CCC. Their common grounding in the use of mindfulness to create distance from both thought and feeling as a means to work on change is discussed, along with their differences. CCC is then set in the context of both the various Third Wave CBT approaches, and of recent developments within psychodynamic therapy that take it in a more collaborative and explicit direction. After reviewing Kath, Tasha and Raju's experience of therapy so far, if any, the chapter concludes by surveying the commonalities between the different therapy modalities, including CCC.

The evolution of therapy

The idea of common humanity and common vulnerability lies at the heart of most therapy approaches. This is the idea that we are all in the same boat, and the water can get rocky; some manage to hang on, while others capsize or go overboard. This perspective fundamentally contradicts the illness model that attributes such capsize to 'illness' or inherent defect. Having said that, many current therapy modalities, including much of CBT, link to specific diagnoses. This is partly to do with the way research is organized, as explained in Chapter 2, and partly to fit in with existing services and gain respectability in the context of medical dominance. It could be argued the IAPT programme would never have secured the commitment and funding that it has achieved in England if it had not linked itself to the NICE guidelines, with their strongly diagnostic organization. It is also a fact that some therapists 'believe' in diagnosis. However, others do not, or recognize their limitations. Trans-diagnostic approaches are gaining traction, especially in the Third Wave therapies (see below).

DOI: 10.4324/9781003081616-4

To return to the challenge of common humanity/common vulnerability, and starting with Freud and the early psychodynamic, psychoanalytic authorities: a particularly challenging aspect of that revolution in thinking was the idea that everyone has murky depths to their psyche, and that, moreover, these depths are frequently the real determinants of action, taking precedence over rational deliberation. This insight represented a major step forward in human thought. Along with Charles Darwin and others' uncovering of humankind's evolutionary journey through the species, it constituted a toppling of 19th century complacency, ushering in the more tortured and uncertain landscape of the 20th century and beyond. Appreciating the hidden depths of the psyche and the importance of emotional life was a major advance in human thought that was experienced as unsettling and challenging by contemporaries.

Indeed, what started to become clear, through techniques that stripped away the veneer of the socially presented persona to reveal the inner turmoil, could be unsettling for the analysts themselves. It seems that Freud could not face up to the revelation that a proportion of his class, including acquaintances, were likely to be abusing, or had abused, their children (Masson 1984). The Oedipus Complex, developed to square this embarrassing circle, was among the first of a succession of complicated mechanisms and theories developed by the psychoanalysts, who held sway in the field of therapy for the first half of the twentieth century. Ideas such as the internalization of early relationships, concealed in Melanie Klein's obscure 'object relations' terminology endure; others such as Klein's emphasis on 'fantasy', which invalidates real life events, has not. Psychoanalysis and other psychodynamic approaches tend to be very hierarchical and expert led. The therapist makes interpretations that the patient receives. When the patient objects, this can be labelled 'resistance'.

Challenge to the pioneers

The psychodynamic/psychoanalytic schools of therapy dominated for some decades, with different schools developing, quarrelling, and founding new institutions; creating ever more complex theories about the way the human mind works. The first challenge to this dominance was launched by the behaviourists. The science of learning theory, starting with Pavlov's exploration of classical conditioning through experiments with salivation in dogs, was taken further by Skinner, Watson and others. Much of the basic science was established in the 1920s and 1930s, but started to be applied seriously to therapy from the 1950s. In the UK, Eysenck (1960) led the way, following the research conducted by Pavlov, Watson and Hull, while Skinner's ideas (Skinner 1974) were applied to therapy in the US. The basic principle that behaviour is maintained and shaped by its consequences and antecedents endures, but the way it was applied to therapy in those early days can now seem simplistic and even dehumanizing. However, the behaviourists' commitment to research and evaluating outcomes was important in establishing the principle that therapy, particularly as delivered by public health services, needs to prove its effectiveness.

Further challenges to the analysts were offered by the humanistic therapies, and then, Cognitive Therapy. Humanistic approaches were grounded in experience and took the body seriously. Carl Rogers' (1951, 1961) Person Centred Psychotherapy was perhaps the most enduringly influential of the humanistic approaches. In contrast to the psychodynamic daunting apparatus of theory, and the mechanistic stance of the early behaviourists, Rogers advocated open-minded listening with unconditional positive regard. The therapist only needed to reflect the individual's experience and trust the client's own innate wisdom to be able to make sense of it, and the individual would find their own way forward. This is recognized now among the myriad therapy modalities as a brilliant place to start from. It helps establish trust and therapeutic alliance. However, it does not always lead to positive change. Where the person's ways of managing life are too set for them to reliably find the way out with no further direction, it can simply serve to entrench them further.

The behaviourists had reacted against what they regarded as the unscientific and ungrounded theorizing of the psychodynamic schools, which led them to ban any sort of introspection or speculation about interior events. This ruled out consideration of cognition. Cognitive Therapy (CT), in contrast, asserted that internally arrived at meaning was a vital intervening variable for human beings, and one that required intervention; that attention to beliefs and meaning could be a counter to irrational, emotionally driven, action. Beck (1976) and Ellis (1962), the main pioneers, had differences in emphasis, but together laid the foundations for an influential new school. Cognitive Behaviour Therapy (CBT) results from adding the power of actually doing things differently to the effects of thinking differently. For instance, anxiety commonly leads to avoidance, and in treating avoidance, it has been found to be far more effective if graded exposure to the avoided situation (actually going back to the supermarket where the panic occurred) is added to challenging the fears at a thinking level (Mattick & Peters 1988).

Behaviour Therapy, CT and CBT have common grounding in behavioural science, and an empirical stance that leads to rigorous evaluation of process and outcome. The resulting 'evidence base' has put them in a strong position in rivalry for dominance with humanistic and psychodynamic competitors. However, that is not their only claim to pre-eminence. Beckian CT and CBT have adopted some of the Rogerian principles of forging a collaborative therapeutic alliance through listening and taking the perspective of the individual seriously, before intervening. In both these therapies the client is an informed and active participant in the change process; they are required to do 'homework' between sessions, and are fully informed about and consenting to the process. This represents a contrast with both humanistic and psychodynamic approaches, where the therapist, so to speak, holds all the cards. It also enables a more transparently contracted, time-limited, therapy. This makes it a practical option for delivery in public health services, such as the NHS.

Third Wave CBT and fitting CCC into the theoretical landscape

Because of its ability to demonstrate success, and its suitability for easily understood, time-limited therapy, CBT has become the most widely available modality, and has continued to develop.

The success of CBT and, for instance, its adoption by the large scale IAPT programme, introduced across England in 2007, has not been without its critics (e.g. Loewenthal & Proctor 2018). Notwithstanding, the modality has forged ahead, taking in its stride the more challenging mental health presentations, those labelled as psychosis, 'personality disorder' and so on. In doing so, it has adapted; it has spread out its tentacles: mopping up priorities such as past experience and the therapeutic relationship that had been the preserve of other modalities, as well as going back to its roots in re-embracing behaviour as opposed to cognition, and above all, appropriating from Buddhism the concept of mindfulness.

I will first cover some of the main Third Wave CBT approaches and then look at where CCC fits in. As suggested above, they all tend to spill out beyond pure CBT, by straying beyond the here and now and emphasizing emotion and relationship. There are advantages to maintaining some connection with CBT, however divergent the actual practice becomes, because of the credibility that CBT confers and its degree of penetration in the NHS in the UK, and beyond. The adherence is not purely cynical, however, as all these approaches retain the CBT characteristics of respectful collaboration, transparency and explicitness. CCC values all these elements at the same time as delving into emotional life and all aspects of relationship; intra- and inter-psychic; i.e. relationship with self, others and the parts within the self. The emphasis on relationship and emotion can feel quite psychodynamic. Likewise, CCC's foundation in felt sense fits well with humanistic therapy.

As well as this distinctiveness, CCC integrates elements from several of the Third Wave CBT modalities, first and foremost from Dialectical Behaviour Therapy (DBT: Linehan 1993). It also takes from Acceptance and Commitment Therapy (ACT: Hayes, Strosahl & Wilson 1999) and Compassion Focused Therapy (CFT: Gilbert 2005), as well as making central use of behavioural analysis. The CCC formulation, in particular, can be used in conjunction with these other approaches as well as with straight CBT. It can further be argued that ICS, the scientific foundation for CCC, has a place, albeit an unacknowledged one, in the development of the Third Wave, to which I will now turn.

The term 'Third Wave' was coined by Steve Hayes, founder of ACT, but the defining feature of the Third Wave is the adoption of mindfulness as a central tool for working on change. Mindfulness leads to a shift in emphasis from the CBT position of seeking to influence the emotion at the heart of the problem (sadness – depression, fear – anxiety disorders, etc.) by altering thoughts and behaviour, towards one of building a new, more flexible, relationship with both thoughts and emotions, thereby loosening their grip on behaviour. Kabat-Zinn (1996) started the movement with his highly successful and thoroughly researched programmes applying mindfulness to problems of stress and pain. This demonstrated both the efficacy and the acceptability within therapy of a technique that had previously been confined to the sphere spiritual practice. This success led to its wide adoption in new therapy approaches: Mindfulness Based Cognitive Therapy (MBCT: Segal, Williams and Teasdale 2002), ACT and DBT to name the main ones.

The role of mindfulness follows naturally from ICS, the model of brain architecture at the heart of CCC, introduced in Chapter 1. Teasdale, one of ICS's founders, was drawn to mindfulness, both because it accorded with his Buddhist practice and because it offered the perfect way to manage that gulf between the two central meaning making systems of ICS, for which we have so far used the DBT terminology of Emotion Mind and Reasonable Mind. Indeed, the diagram at the heart of the DBT formulation of the human condition, the States of Mind diagram, neatly encapsulates this split (Figure 1.1), and is adopted, with the addition of memory, by CCC.

DBT was developed for suicidal and self-harming women, but has seen its application significantly widened. DBT uses mindfulness in a more flexible and less rigorous fashion than Kabat-Zinn and MBCT: the latter stuck more closely to its roots in Buddhist practice. DBT also introduces the concept of skills deficit and skills training with regard to emotions. DBT links individual therapy with group training. Furthermore, delivery of the manualized training does not require the same level of specialization as the individual therapy, opening the way to a distributed model of therapy delivery. DBT has a tight way of organizing this in its four modes of treatment offered concurrently: individual therapy, skills training, telephone consultation and case consultation for therapists (Linehan 1993, p. 101). Within CCC, the Cope and Connect arms of the therapy take the form of skills teaching in order to develop new ways of coping with that intolerable felt sense that is always the starting point. DBT techniques for managing emotion are particularly relevant here.

Acceptance and Commitment Therapy (ACT) is about diffusing thoughts and feelings from action and sense of agency, and taking control of that agency in the pursuit of individual values. ACT's emphasizes the role of values in helping the individual to rise above familiar, stuck patterns of behaviour and grasp motivation to accept unwelcome reality, unpleasant emotions, and the challenge of moving into uncharted territory. The values aspect of ACT is incorporated into CCC.

As the name suggests, developing self-compassion is central to Paul Gilbert's Compassion Focused Therapy (CFT: Gilbert 2005), and this fits seamlessly with CCC emphasis on the self/self-relationship, of which more in the next chapter. Paul Gilbert's thinking is founded on an evolutionary perspective, already noted with reference to depression. This perspective recognizes the fundamentally social nature of the human being which can get lost in our individualistic culture. Hierarchical social organization is written into our make-up, and our internal felt sense registers our position in that hierarchy. Affiliation is natural and essential to our functioning and well-being, so that its disruption, whether past or present, inevitably causes emotional distress (Gilbert 1992). All these basic realities, recognized by CFT, are fundamental for CCC.

Integrative psychodynamic approaches

Meanwhile, parallel developments were taking place among some psychodynamic approaches (others remain firmly rooted in the past). The three psychodynamic or integrative approaches that are most closely linked to CCC are: Attachment, (e.g. Bowlby 1988, Ainsworth et al. 1978) Mentalization-Based Treatment (MBT, Bateman & Fonagy 2004) and Cognitive Analytic Therapy, CAT (Ryle & Kerr 2004). Most psychodynamic therapies have theoretical bases which link formative early experience to the development of the self and to later adaptation. Attachment theory was probably the first to found these conclusions on systematic study of infant/caregiver relationships, which gives it solidity as compared to the wilder speculations of, say, Kleinian theory. The idea that internalized patterns of relationship are the bedrock of the self fits well with the CCC idea that, when Emotion Mind is in the ascendant, we are relationship – to a greater or lesser extent. CAT captures this incorporation of experience of relationship through the very useful concept of the Reciprocal Role.

Reciprocal Roles are traced in the process of CAT formulation, with an emphasis on their two-way operation. For instance, the individual who has been abused will have internalized an 'abuser-abused' reciprocal role. Either pole of that role can be acted out in their subsequent relationships until they learn to identify and revise the pattern. CAT was influential in the development of CCC and there are some overlaps. The operation of dysfunctional reciprocal roles invariably results in aversive emotions – in other words, they feed the horrible feeling. The more cognitive arm of CAT then picks up the resulting coping patterns in its menu of procedures, which can map onto CCC's simpler maintaining cycles.

Mentalization is important for CCC in that it mirrors the DBT approach of identifying skills deficit and teaching skills, utilized in the post formulation section of CCC. In the case of MBT, the skills are focused on interpersonal relating and developing theory of mind, which usefully complements the more individually focused DBT skills.

More generally, CCC's acknowledgement of the powerful role of emotion, the complexity of emotions where a surface emotion masks a deeper one, and the limitations of cognition and conscious processing, accord with a psychodynamic perspective. However, the strictly collaborative, here and now, and behavioural emphasis of CCC contrasts with many psychodynamic approaches apart from the more integrative examples such as CAT and MBT.

Kath, Tasha and Raju's experience with therapy (if any) so far

Kath had received a long course of CBT for depression about ten years previously, and has had some input from IAPT since; initially in the form of guided self-help. This did not have much impact, so was followed by a further course of individual CBT for depression. CBT taught her to challenge her negative view of herself, and she manages to use this when the depression is not too deep. When she feels really down, she cannot keep this up, and simply feels guilty as she is aware that she is thinking 'wrong'.

As related earlier, Tasha's diagnosis has not led to any straightforward treatment solution. Counselling from Child and Adolescent services did not have any great impact. Following her move to adult services, there have been attempts to engage her in the DBT service, which specializes in this diagnosis, but she has been unwilling (or unable?) to make the required commitment.

Raju has not yet been seen by any health professional.

Commonalities between the therapies

There are certain over-arching commonalities between these various therapy modalities that have been surveyed.

Sense making and formulation

All the modalities recognize, in some form, a human need to make sense of the situation in a manner that offers a better way forward. In many varieties of CBT, and in CAT, this leads to the construction of an individual formulation, sometimes, but not always in the form of a diagram. Such a formulation diagram is central for CCC, with some overlap and some differences with, for instance, CAT and CBT diagrams.

Relationship

Relationship is almost always given prominence in therapy. This ranges on a continuum from recognition of the need to build a good therapeutic alliance with trust and warmth in order to get anywhere, to an expectation that the person encountered in the therapy room will re-enact the past relationships that are the building blocks of their present self (and so, if not vigilant, the therapist may be drawn into the re-enactment): transference, to use psychodynamic terminology. The extent to which this is the focus of the therapy varies across modalities.

The self/self-relationship

Whether or not the relationship that the individual has with themselves is an explicit focus (as is in CCC and CAT), it is always at the heart of mental health difficulties. The depressed person puts themselves down and neglects themselves; the self-harmer attacks themselves; the anorexic starves themselves, and so on. Healing starts with healing this self/self-relationship; accepting yourself just as you are along with the situation in which you find yourself – as a starting point to work for something better. It is the role of the therapist to model that compassionate but honest relationship and so provide this starting point.

The role of trauma in current difficulties

This is given more prominence in some modalities than in others, but is always in the background. Some favour revisiting and 'reliving' the past; others prefer to work in the present. DBT introduced the idea, now widely accepted, that revisiting highly emotionally charged areas without sufficient skills and stability to manage the emotions is a recipe for destabilization. CCC is explicit about naming trauma as a crucial factor in the present, while not requiring the person to revisit anything they do not feel ready for, and substitutes building a new, healthy, relationship with the accepted past rather than explore it.

Conclusion and summary

This chapter has attempted to sketch in the landscape of therapy. We have seen how the psychoanalysts and psychodynamic theorists and therapists from early in the 20th century opened the interior of the mind to exploration and speculation; how the more scientific, behavioural and cognitive behavioural approaches both reacted against the speculation and worked to put the practice of supporting human beings towards beneficial change on a more scientific basis. The humanistic schools reminded these more austere disciplines of the importance of the human relationship at the heart of therapy, whether used as a tool for change in its own right, or as a basis for challenge to the status quo.

Following the success of CBT in capturing the high ground, certainly in terms of publicly funded therapy provision, because of its commitment to transparency and evaluation, we saw how the Third Wave developed CBT, sometimes almost out of all recognition, adding elements of value to the therapeutic process from every direction.

CCC fits neatly as an integration between the individual formulation favoured by CAT and much CBT, and the skills-based approaches found in DBT and MBT. It uses mindfulness (in a light touch form, closely allied to grounding) as a medium of change, which aligns it with the rest of the Third Wave, along with an emphasis on behaviour as opposed to cognition. It gives prominence to relationship, in particular the self/self-relationship, and is trauma-informed.

However, its foundation in ICS gives it other, more unique features. The centrality of felt sense, emotion and ultimately, the body, moves it in a more humanistic direction. Its perspective on relationship, and spirituality/altered states of consciousness, to be explored in the next chapter, is another departure. The bold ICS claim that 'there is no boss' leads to a radical revision of the notion of the self, from something unquestioningly accepted, to a shifting sands. In the next chapter we will explore that claim and its ramifications, in terms of the self, constituted from and maintained by relationship. This will pave the way for considering the potential to step beyond the self and to experience more than we can precisely know.

4 Falling between the cracks

Self, relationship, spirituality and mental health

Introductory summary

This is the chapter where key ideas that have already been introduced in outline will be given more thorough treatment. Central among these is the CCC view of the self as process, or to put it another way, as shifting sands. This will necessitate a fuller exposition of the ICS model of cognitive architecture and its roots in human evolution. This exposition paves the way for considering the far-reaching implications of the model, which fall into several categories. The instability and inherent incompleteness of the individual is one. Allied to this is the way that relationships form a major constituent of our being. At the same time, it is our important relationships that provide the containment necessary for us to function in the world. Relationship with other human beings is only the starting point, as the concept of relationship here broadens out to include the roles that knit us together with others, and relationship with our wider environment. Our crucial dependency on these external props becomes apparent when they falter or fail, with adverse effects on our internal state. It is then that our attempts to maintain a good enough internal state can make matters worse, hence the human propensity to break down.

This perspective situates each individual within an ever-widening web of relationship. These relationships, many of which we pay no heed to, have a critical effect upon our internal state. Within this web, we are bound up with the society of which we are a part, meaning that we have little control over crucial relationships. An important example is the destructive relationship with the planet on which we depend. The fact that it is our society's destructive relationship with the earth does not save us individually from both the internal, in terms of felt sense, and the more obvious external consequences of that destructiveness.

Finally, this ICS-based viewpoint provides a way of understanding the enduring sense of spiritual connection, and for many, of faith, in a secular age. This is linked to the property of our divided processing that gives us two distinct ways of knowing. This can enable humans to step 'beyond the threshold' into a different quality of experience; one that can be variously feted as mysticism or shunned as madness. This implication will be explored more fully in Chapter 8.

DOI: 10.4324/9781003081616-5

Return to assumption busting – the illusion of self-sufficiency

Freud and the psychoanalysts succeeded in smashing complacency around the degree of control we have over our lives with the concepts of the subconscious/unconscious. Interacting Cognitive Subsystems (ICS), the theoretical model that underpins CCC that was introduced in Chapter 1, enables us to take this further. This will be explored in this chapter, along with far-reaching implications for understanding not just mental breakdown, but human beings and their place in the world.

The psychodynamic argument that the real determinant of our actions and therefore our lives lies beneath the surface is nicely summed up by the philosopher, Daniel Dennett (1983, p. 79), saying that, if the human being was a business, the conscious experience of self would be not so much the managing director as the person in charge of public relations; the man or woman in the press office who doesn't necessarily know what is really going on but has to present a spin on it, favourable to the reputation of the organization. Even at a conscious level, we can recognize the way that the internal dialogue constantly constructs events into the acceptable (interesting? Amusing?) 'story' to present both to ourselves and to the rest of the world. This argument is here taken further, based on the two distinct ways of knowing indicated by ICS, to call into question both the internal coherence and the external absolute boundedness of the individual.

To start with the internal aspect, it has already been suggested that it is the emotional mind (see Figure 1.1), operating below the radar, that determines many of our decisions and actions. Emotion mind and reasonable mind working together (wise mind) then take in the impact of these decisions and actions within the wider context, coming up with a plausible story in retrospect; one that will best preserve our status in the world (i.e. within our relevant primate hierarchy) and hence preserve a tolerable sense of self and internal state.

This process, which happens all the time, requires seamless transition between the dominance of emotional and wise minds. However, as we have seen, at high and at low arousal, this smooth transfer of control breaks down, and emotion mind remains dominant. When emotion mind takes charge in this way, the very boundaries of our individuality can become porous. A picture of the human being that is loosely held together, a constant transaction between two organizing centres (emotion mind and reasonable mind) starts to emerge. This picture makes the prevalence of mental breakdown and malfunction all the easier to understand, and more normal. It also becomes clear that our subjective sense of a self in control is a (very convenient) illusion.

Return to ICS

In order to argue this point, it is necessary to go into the ICS model of cognitive architecture in a bit more detail. ICS was worked out precisely through computer modelling and closely based on the findings of a couple of decades of detailed cognitive research into human information processing and memory – examining the bottlenecks, coding modalities, and other experimentally established features of thinking and memory. This modelling identified nine distinct subsystems, each managing a different aspect of human functioning, such as the different senses, or the verbal and vocal apparatus, for instance. Crucially, the model demonstrates that they are organized into two central meaning making systems, hitherto referred to as emotion mind and reasonable mind. Within ICS, emotion mind is known as the Implicational Subsystem, and reasonable mind as the Propositional Subsystem. They remain distinct, but in a normal state of arousal, constantly communicate via what ICS calls 'the central engine of cognition'. This is equivalent to the DBT 'Wise Mind'.

The development of this singular brain organization is explained in terms of the modifications to the simpler, single overarching organizing system, of the basic ape brain, required by evolution. Our species needed to adapt to the management of increasingly complex data as we evolved from primates similar to chimpanzees towards the early hominids and then Homo Sapiens. Precise manipulation of tools made possible by the opposing thumb and forefinger, (Barnard 2010), and the development of more sophisticated communication amongst a larger group through language, were the identified drivers of the need for the central processing system to split into two, in order to manage the new complexity.

So much is generally understood. Less widely appreciated is the way in which this interchange between two organizing systems, or circuits in the brain, produces the two separate ways in which we encounter reality – or whatever is out there. In our normal mode of operation, with the propositional and implicational co-operating to exchange information regularly, we can interact with our environment in a very exact way. This is made possible because our perception is filtered. The exactitude obtains over a limited range, but we are generally unaware of the limits, which are normally beyond our current focus. (These limits start to become apparent within the physics of the very small and the very large, as in Quantum Theory and Cosmology.) This filtered, limited perception gives us the ordinary way of knowing. However, when the implicational takes charge and the propositional is no longer able to perform its filtering and focusing function, we start to experience the world beyond, and to experience in a different way. Thus, each way of knowing has a distinct character; each has its strengths and its limitations. However, because of the way that our brains smooth over anything that does not quite match up, as explained in Chapter 1, we are normally unaware of this 'crack'.

The difference in character between the two can be understood in terms of the pathways that connect or do not connect the different bits of the brain. The newer processing system, the one that split off in response to evolutionary pressure, reasonable mind which in DBT terminology; 'the propositional' in ICS, connects directly with the parts of the brain to do with speech production. The propositional gives us our capacity for precise thinking; our ability to discriminate and work things out. In conjunction with the other main subsystem, the implicational or emotion mind, it enables us to grasp the bigger picture. The two main subsystems working together in this way represent the slow, cool calm and collected mode of thought. I propose that it is the pro-positional that facilitates the experience of individual self-consciousness that arguably distinguishes us from our other primate ancestors.

The other processing system, the implicational or emotion mind, organizes all the rest – the senses and the body's arousal system. It receives sensory information from the outside world and grasps its significance for the self. Survival is of course the number one priority, and next to that, social position within the primate hierarchy. Relationship is basic to both of these. The baby only survives where it is held in a nurturing relationship, and relationship and status within the wider group become increasingly important as the child grows to adulthood. These crucial aspects of our humanity are governed by emotions that link sense perception with the body's state of arousal in order to trigger action. Where the sense information spells danger, the body switches mode into action stations; where we experience loving relations and nurturing, our body feels calm and affiliative (Gilbert 2005). In evolutionary terms, it is understandable that the system responding to threat should have the capacity to override the other one. For modern life, it is that very override that spells trouble.

So much should be readily recognizable from our experience. Normal life of course needs the information from both of these systems to make sense of and navigate the world, so we rely on them to constantly exchange information; an exchange that, according to ICS, does not have an overall 'self' or 'I' in charge. 'I' am wherever the constantly fluctuating system happens to have landed for the moment, and the sense of self is built up over time from the shifting sands of experience and relationship.

Normal life is characterized by smooth cooperation between these two meaning making systems, but at high and at low arousal, they separate, and the implicational, which is the default system, takes charge. This happens in states of high emotion and stress, but also when we are asleep, or our mind is drift-ing. The role of memory within the ICS system has already been alluded to in Chapter 1 in explanation for the phenomenon of trauma memory. Impact of trauma will be looked at in more detail in the next chapter.

ICS, self-consciousness and beyond

Seeing the human being at the mercy of a system over which he or she has only partial and fluctuating control makes our propensity to break down all the more comprehensible. From this perspective, the efforts of mental health ser-vices, whether medical or psychotherapeutic, need to be directed towards helping the individual re-assert control in the interests of good functioning. As already mentioned, mindfulness is a good first step towards establishing, how-ever fleetingly, an internal vantage point from which both systems can be observed and co-ordinated.

In some ways this picture parallels the psychodynamic enterprise of bringing into the light of day what the sub- or unconscious is up to. However, we need to be aware that reflecting on consciousness takes us into slippery territory. In Chapter 1, the argument was made that our ability to grasp anything is severely limited by our thinking and perceiving apparatus, but that these very systems are designed to mask awareness of this. Considering these topics, we find ourselves at the mercy of spatial metaphors. 'Subconscious' locates the action below, a sort of cellar within the individual mind. Jung's 'Unconscious' explicitly gets away from the individual focus as it is 'collective', but it is still under. However we try to pin it down, we are dependent on language and the baggage of association that language brings with it.

I prefer the metaphor of 'across' which is somehow less value laden. I suggest that when we move from one way of knowing to another, we step 'beyond' our individuality. The concept of 'losing yourself' in music, a good book, an intense experience, creative activity etc. is commonly understood. Go further; leave the safety of the propositional/reasonable mind further behind, and a different quality of experience is encountered. This is the realm of unusual or anomalous experiences; of mysticism – and madness; beyond the self and beside the self to bring in more metaphor. I find the word coined by Thalbourne (Thalbourne & Delin, 1994) and adopted by Claridge (1997), 'The Transliminal', meaning 'across the threshold', a useful descriptor. Claridge has advanced this whole area of enquiry with his extensive research into Schizotypy or the dimension of openness to unusual experiencing (not to be confused with diagnoses starting with 'schiz').

Leaving these extreme states aside for a moment, the availability of these two ways of knowing, these two modes of being, which most of the time are in a constant state of interchange, offer a new perspective on relationship and the self to which we now turn.

The web of relationship

Attachment Theory, CAT Reciprocal Roles and Kleinian Object Relations theory were alluded to in Chapter 3. Each, in slightly different ways, captures the idea that formative relationships are the building blocks of the human personality. The baby makes sense of both the world and of itself through the reaction of his/her caregivers, internalizing patterns of interaction that it will then enact in relations to others. As the child grows, the variety of these experiences will multiply; the bullies at school; the appreciative teacher. All will add different dimensions of threat and opportunity, to be laid down in the implicational memory and shape the development of the child. This takes place in interaction with the child's intrinsic temperament, though research into childhood adversity demonstrates that the raised cortisol levels produced by the stress of abuse and neglect sets up a lifetime of greater emotional reactivity (van der Kolk 2014, Schore 1994), so that even this is influenced by environment.

The complexity deepens when we realize that each of the people with whom the child relates are themselves influenced by the relationships and environment around them. The parent might be unavailable to the child because of the pressure of needing to earn enough money in a harsh employment environment, insecurities around accommodation or benefits. These pressures might have proved intolerable, and drink, gambling, drugs, etc. might have offered escape, further cutting off their

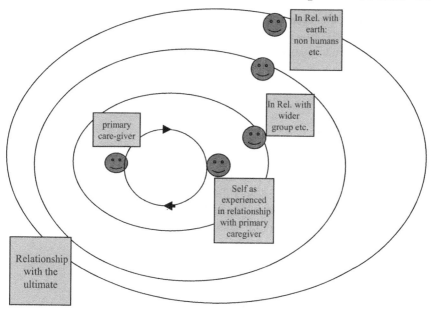

Figure 4.1 Web of Relationships

availability to relate to, and care for, the child. Even where external circumstances are more favourable, the limitations might come from the parent's own experience of inadequate or abusive parenting, again driven by adverse environments.

These circles of relatedness spread wider still. Our sense of who we are in the world is shaped by relationship to our group, our class, profession, nation as well as our family. Then there is relationship with more distant people; those who make and ship our goods from afar; the migrants who seek our shores because the places they come from have been destroyed or become inhospitable through war and climate change; the far-reaching tentacles of colonialism; relationship with the earth, and the other species with which we share it. Figure 4.1 is an attempt to convey all this.

Some relationships are sound and nurturing, but many, particularly the ones we don't spend much time thinking about, are problematic. I am arguing that, when we move from close interchange between propositional and implicational, we move away from being centred in our individual self-consciousness. We progressively move beyond our individuality into a place of experiencing ourselves as relationship; all the relationships enumerated above and more. This means that the nature of these relationships is significant for us. Where they are distorted and abusive (as for instance our relationship with the earth), even if we don't think about it, it still affects the core of our being. It could be that the pain this engenders sets up a vulnerability to turn to behaviours that numb feeling; the obvious addictions, but also things we take for granted like consumption – shopping. This argument is well developed by the theologian, Matthew Fox (1983).

Not only do relationships constitute us in this very real sense; they are also the glue that holds each of us together as a functioning individual, hence their importance in understanding mental health breakdown. Breakdown characteristically occurs at times of loss or life transition. The teenager leaves home for job or study; the individual suffers a major bereavement; or loss of role through losing employment or retirement, or migration – and the many other life events that remove familiar supports. The devastating effect of this loss, or change in circumstances, is the evidence that these relationships and roles have hitherto been important constituents of our sense of self. With their removal, this can crumble, leading to emotional desperation. This desperation might easily be managed in ways that make sense in the short term (shutting down, ruminative worry, drink or drugs) but lead further into loss of functioning, deeper distress – and mental health diagnosis.

In summary, recognizing that human beings are both constituted and contained by this web of relationship goes a long way to understanding our susceptibility to breakdown.

Spiritual connection and mental health

There is another sort of relationship that has been experienced by humans throughout the ages. This is a sense of connection, often intimate connection, with that which is beyond, intangible, all powerful, sometimes benevolent and merciful, sometimes vengeful and judging. This relationship goes under many different names – relationship with God, Goddess, Spirit, or devolved to others such as Buddha, Jesus, Mohammed. This relationship is named as the widest circle in Figure 4.1, but could equally be seen as the deepest.

This widest/deepest relationship can give a sense of anchoring in an unforgiving world, a sense of belonging and purpose, a moral compass; the possibility of healing and reversing the perpetuation of abuse outlined above. People have wasted energy over the millennia arguing about names, characters, existence or non-existence. I suggest that in the transliminal (across the threshold) way of knowing, we have to accept the sense of relationship as valid data, but also accept the fact that it can extend beyond our capacity for precise knowing, and indeed for verbal naming. All verbal precision belongs to the propositional, and this sort of knowing has left the propositional far behind.

However, the experiential, relational way of knowing is real and powerful, so that this ultimate, 'divine', relationship can still constitute an important part of us. Maybe the sense of specialness, which seems universal, even when given no support by real world relationships, as in the case of people who have suffered severe abuse, comes from that underlying relationship. It is not necessary for the relationship to be explicitly recognized for it to have powerful effect.

Conclusion and summary

This chapter has delved more deeply into the theory of Interacting Cognitive Subsystems in order to demonstrate the impact that the existence of two central meaning making systems, the implicational and propositional, with alternating control, has on the human vulnerability to breakdown. This way in which our brains have evolved both gives us the faculties of precise control (within a prescribed compass) and sophisticated communication, but also involves limitations. The problem is that our brains are designed to disguise the limitations, so that we can remain unaware of them, and of the potential that can open up when we step 'beyond the threshold'.

The interchange between the systems opens the way to the role that relationship plays in our internal state and in our sense of who we are. The nature of the relationships within which we are entangled, often beyond our awareness and control, impacts our internal state – that 'felt sense' that is crucial for our wellbeing (Chapter 1). The key part played by the central roles and relationships in our life for our good functioning becomes evident when they are removed.

Spirituality and faith are recognized as a further circle of relationship, and one that can become important when the others crumble. All in all, mental breakdown comes to appear a more understandable, and even normal, aspect of being human.

In the next chapter we will consider another central factor in that vulnerability to breakdown; the way in which the implicational, our emotion mind, does not understand time, which is the province of the propositional. When the two are not communicating, the implicational will link past threat situations with current ones, with dire consequences for our internal state. In this way, past trauma plays a central role in much mental distress.

5 Trauma and mental breakdown

Introductory summary

The role of memory for past threat experiences and trauma in mental distress has already been introduced. Its importance for normalizing the experience of breakdown by explaining how events that happened years or decades previously can intensify challenging experiences, often completely different in nature, in the present, has been clarified. In this chapter, the phenomenon of the intrusion of the past into the present through the memory is explored in more depth. The evidence about different types of memory emerging from research is introduced, and matched with the ICS model of cognitive architecture. The traditional way in which trauma is treated within both psychodynamic and CBT therapy is then considered before explaining the distinct, CCC, approach to trauma. The chapter ends with a return to the three illustrative cases. More about their past history and significant relationships is now revealed, so that the picture of what led to their respective breakdowns starts to become clearer.

The presence of the past

In Chapter 1 we introduced the idea that the emotion mind (implicational) memory preserved memory of threat, along with bodily mobilization to deal with it, divorced from context. Context, including time and place, are provided by the reasonable mind (propositional) when the two meaning making systems are in good communication. When high arousal takes over, because of threat in the present, they drift apart. This gives access to experience of threat across time; the body responds to this accumulation of supposed threat, thus intensifying the sense of threat in the present. This vicious cycle provides the mechanism whereby distant trauma becomes a potent factor in current breakdown.

This summary, based on the ICS model of brain architecture, is borne out by the extensive research into types of memory carried out by Chris Brewin and his colleagues. This team propose a distinction in types of memory that mirrors the ICS dichotomy; their 'verbally accessible memory' or VAM can be recognized as the propositional memory; their 'situationally accessible memory' or SAM (Brewin, Dalgleish & Joseph 1996, Brewin 2001) mirrors the implicational

DOI: 10.4324/9781003081616-6

memory. Their experimental studies found robust evidence of association between strong emotion and vivid recall, divorced from time and context (Brewin 2018, 2011). These memories home in on the threat that was experienced, along with seemingly irrelevant but sharply recalled details that somehow get caught up with it, without giving a coherent sense of what was happening in general. Unpredictable triggers can re-ignite these powerful memories, disrupting life in the present with an unwelcome flashback. Brewin and his colleagues' research provides a coherent explanation for the disorienting experience of the Post Traumatic Stress Disorder (PTSD) sufferer's experience of being plunged into reliving in the present, a traumatic experience from the past, whether of combat trauma, near fatal accident, or other dire circumstance.

From these findings, it can be inferred that memory for a coherent narrative requires constant interchange between the propositional and the implicational, and this is seriously disrupted by the high arousal associated with trauma and prolonged threat. Where the experience in the present is unbearable, the natural defence mechanism is to dissociate – not to take it in. The split between the two main subsystems makes this easy – you just decouple the propositional or VAM. The threat memory thus remains, locked in the implicational, which hangs onto it because it carries important information about danger which could be handy for keeping you safe in the future, but in a disjointed and fragmentary form. Where this happens repeatedly, it plays havoc with the individual's ability to reconstruct a joined-up narrative of their past – or autobiographical memory as it is labelled in the research literature. Further research explores how autobiographical memory is impaired in people who have experienced repeated trauma (Williams et al. 2007). Their recall of their past is over general, and lacks the richness of detail, lost in the effort to defend against the unbearable.

Therapy and memory for trauma

This phenomenon has long been recognized within the different schools of therapy and the general consensus is that the past trauma, which is being re-experienced minus its context, needs re-connection with its context; in other words, implicational and propositional information needs to be brought together. This has traditionally involved 'reliving'; telling the story of the traumatic memories to a sympathetic and validating therapist, who will encourage the individual to dwell on the emotional 'hotspots' (Grey, Holmes & Brewin 2001). The therapist invites them to revise the original meaning, or challenge the surrounding cognitions (depending on the modality of the therapy), and link back to the reality of safety in the present. There are differences in emphasis between psychodynamic and CBT approaches. Psychodynamic approaches (e.g. Wilson & Thomas 2004, Brom, Kleber & Defares 1989) emphasize the therapeutic relationship and re-experiencing the feelings. CBT (e.g. Ehlers & Clark 2000) emphasizes challenging the thoughts that give clue to the meaning assigned to the events, but essentially the approach is very similar.

Because it entails revisiting distressing material, this is inevitably a challenging process, and not everyone is ready to open the Pandora's box. Techniques such as EMDR (Shapiro & Maxfield 2002) can help, but it is recognized that some people cannot contain safely the intense emotions released. DBT, for instance, insists that people severely affected by past trauma should spend a year intensively learning skills to manage these emotions before embarking on reliving.

Notwithstanding these difficulties, the importance of taking the impact of trauma seriously is now generally recognized. The evidence uncovering the prevalence of trauma among people receiving mental health diagnoses, cited in Chapter 1, has become inescapable. This was first acknowledged and investigated in the case of so-called 'personality disorder' (Masson et al. 2013). It came to be recognized that the sort of impulsive behaviours that invited this diagnosis were attempts to manage the unbearable emotional state produced by earlier, usually prolonged and repeated, trauma. The characteristic difficulties with relationships could often be traced back to confusing, unreliable and abusive earlier experiences of relationship. Consequently, it has been suggested that a better label would be 'complex trauma'.

For those with an investment in upholding the survival of a pure, biological, 'mental illness' conceptualization, maintaining a clear distinction between so-called personality disorder and psychosis was important, until even this certainty started to be eroded. Evidence for earlier trauma in a significant proportion of psychosis sufferers is gathering (Read, Bentall & Fosse 2009). With the growing realization of the ubiquity of trauma in mental health presentations, the concept of 'trauma-informed' services has become increasingly wide-spread.

Trauma-informed services were first developed in the USA, and a paper by Sweeney, Clement, Filson & Kennedy (2016) reviews the concept and its prevalence in the UK. As well as citing the need for such services because of the proven link between trauma and mental health, and our growing understanding of the neurological effects of repeated trauma on development, the authors point to the danger of re-traumatization by mental health services that do not take trauma into account. This occurs unintentionally in a variety of ways, whether through failure to acknowledge the effects of trauma, or conversely, insensitive questioning about it. Re-traumatization can unfortunately also result through the exercise of power that occurs when someone is involuntarily hospitalized and medicated. To someone who has experienced earlier abuse, this can be yet another violation. The establishment of a Trauma-Informed Approach by the Esk, Tyne & Wear NHS mental health service and the broader recognition of the need for Trauma Aware services in Scotland is a start, but there is still a long way to go.

CCC and trauma

CCC takes the impact of trauma very seriously without advocating reliving. This does not mean that reliving is not going to be important for recovery in some people and it does not exclude the possibility of therapy involving reliving taking place in the future. CCC can be a good preparation for a longer term, in depth, therapy following it. However, for many people, including those who have experienced significant trauma, CCC is an adequate therapy on its own, and a course of CCC is enough for them to turn their lives around and face forwards. If this proves the case, not having to go through the harrowing process of reliving, but instead rebuilding a sound life in the present going into the future, is a preferable alternative. Clarke & Nicholls (2018), who include examples of people who have been through the therapy and given their permission for their stories to be included, present cases which illustrate this (Clare, p. 35; Lisa, p. 82). Taking Lisa's example, her scores on a measure of impact of events were quite high when she entered therapy, which was not surprising as she had been brought up amid violence, and was haunted by the trauma of finding her baby brother, whom she had had a major role caring for, dead when she was only 13. At the end of the 17-session therapy, her score on that measure was 0. It would be good to be able to evaluate and demonstrate this effect more than anecdotally, and this is a future plan.

CCC incorporates trauma as follows. The emotion mind/reasonable mind split is explained early on, along with the way that trauma memory can become decoupled from time. This gives a normalizing and non-blaming explanation for the individual's desperation and consequent attempts to manage (self-harm, drinking, withdrawing, etc.) The past is summarized concisely, but meaningfully, in a box in the formulation diagram, the 'comprehend' part of the programme (Figure 5.1). The box is linked by arrows to both more immediate triggers that might have re-awoken the earlier sense of threat, and to the intolerable emotion at the heart of the diagram, in a way that illustrates clearly how the past has been re-triggered by recent events, and so impacts directly on current difficulties. It is emphasized that because current, understandable, coping strategies (self-harm, etc.) maintain or exacerbate the intolerable feeling, and so keep the person stuck in emotion mind, they will serve to keep the past alive in the present – a good reason for finding alternative ways of managing the emotion.

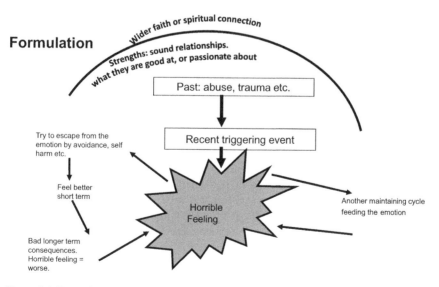

Figure 5.1 Formulation

The intervention phase that follows the formulation has, as one of its components, building a new relationship with the past. This will be covered in detail in Chapter 16, but in summary, mindfulness makes it possible to gain some distance from which to view the past. Having achieved this observer stance, the first task, a formidable one, is to accept what happened. As emphasized in DBT, accepting is not the same as approving, but unless what has occurred is faced and accepted rather than avoided and denied, it will continue to hold power.

The next step is to use key emotions to reshape the relationship to that past. These emotions are compassion, anger and sadness. Compassion is vital for revising the individual's relationship with their past self; for example, in the case of the child who was victimized and has accepted the blame that the abuser laid on them long ago, their adult self needs to view their child self as they would any other child in that situation, and allow themselves to feel compassion for their powerlessness and distress. In the case of the anger, this needs to be brought out, if it has been denied and hidden, and tamed if it is out of control. The anger at what was done, or, in the case of neglect, not done, has packed within it the sense of 'I had a right to better'. There is strength in that acknowledgement of rights, which, coupled with the physical arousal that accompanies anger, can be used to find the courage to face the past, put it in the past, and go forward. It will still be necessary to acknowledge and mourn the good childhood, or other past, that is lost forever, and that is where sadness and tears come in. More will be said about using emotions for healing in this way in subsequent chapters.

Trauma, relationships and spirituality for Kath, Tasha and Raju

Our three examples were not picked up in the last chapter, so I am taking these aspects together, as they are linked. Up until now, we have not had the information needed to fill in this part of the history. This is normal when people first approach mental health services in breakdown and are simply told, for instance, a diagnosis. The crucial details about what happened to them will only emerge once they have had an opportunity to tell their story, which is the first stage of a CCC therapy. Tasha's story comes first, as she illustrates most clearly the impact of recognizable trauma.

Tasha

Tasha's family history was well documented by the mental health services. She had three brothers, and her mother had been involved with several different men over the years. Tasha's own father was well out of the picture. She had been brought up by her nan until, at the age of eight, her mother brought her to live with her and her new partner, an unwelcome move for Tasha. This stepfather sexually abused her between the ages of eight and 11. The abuse was deeply disturbing and traumatizing for Tasha. For years she was too frightened to say anything because of her abuser's threats, and did not think she would be believed because of his powerful place in the family. When she finally overcame the fear, she told her mother, who threw him out, but would not back her up to prosecute, as his friends and relatives were still very much part of their circle.

Another important relationship for Tasha was her disabled younger brother. He suffered from severe learning disabilities. Tasha both felt protective towards him, and was probably the person who was best at understanding and caring for him when he displayed disturbance. She was also very resentful at the way his needs dominated everything and took attention away from her. Tasha was a caring person, deeply involved with her family. Her relations with her mother, who suffered from rheumatoid arthritis and fibromyalgia, were complex. She was at the same time close and protective towards her, and angry and resentful towards her, because of her mother's failure to protect her and preoccupation with the disabled brother.

Kath

In contrast to Tasha, Kath had not suffered trauma in childhood. That came later. However, her parents had been relatively emotionally unavailable. Her father was cold, critical and controlling, and her mother, a much warmer and gentler person, was too much under her husband's control and miserable in the relationship to provide much of a counterweight. Kath escaped from this home situation into an early marriage that started well, but soon proved abusive. Domestic violence became an issue with her pregnancy, and she had to escape to a women's refuge and temporary housing. Once she found somewhere settled to live and a job, she devoted her life to caring for her daughter. Her mother tried to be a support, within the limits allowed by Kath's father.

Recently, however, Kath had ventured into another relationship, which proved more disastrous than the first. While she recognized the signs and sought to end it fairly rapidly, she was being harassed and pursued by this individual, and lived in fear of him. At the same time, her mother was experiencing the early signs of dementia and Kath was desperately worried by her father's inability to care compassionately in this situation. All these factors created considerable stress. Kath had a faith, but had drifted away from the church. Through all of this, Kath's relationship with her 12-year-old daughter was the most constant and important one in her life.

Raju

Raju was not very communicative when he first met his therapist. He was taken up with his own preoccupations and could not see the point of talking about the past. However, he attended an appointment with Ambika, who was acutely aware of the pressures on her husband when he was growing up and later and was able to relate the story. The youngest by seven years of five brothers, his parents were loving, but his powerful father expected all his sons to follow in his footsteps and become successful businessmen. The four eldest, close in age and character, did. Raju was different from the start; slighter in build, sensitive, with artistic talent from an early age, and a growing interest in philosophy. His brothers resented their parents', as they saw it, indulgence of their younger brother and bullied him; an experience that was repeated with racist overtones at school.

Though charmed by the intricate and unusual patterns he created in his artwork, his father would not hear of it as a career, or philosophy as a subject of study. Raju was also gifted at maths, so studied that at university, where his passion for pure maths, with its aesthetic side, would have destined him for an academic career in this field. Because such a course inevitably started insecurely, his father insisted on accountancy, which would equip him to contribute to the family business. He was about to be married to Ambika, a partner identified by the families but also a real love match for the couple, and he had to have a solid career. More bullying, unhappiness and failure to fit in at work followed, and while his career faltered, both families were impatient for offspring. When he lost his last job, Ambika suggested he combine some freelance work with becoming a house husband and take on childcare, so that they could start a family while she pursued her successful career, but Raju angrily declined. She guessed he feared the reaction of his father and brothers. More will emerge about Raju's relationship with spirituality later.

Conclusion and summary

This chapter has tackled the role of trauma and past adversity in mental health challenges. ICS offers an easily graspable model to explain how past memory for threat can play such an intrusive part in the emotional life of the present, and this enables people to understand their own breakdown in a normalizing fashion. They recognize that what they are experiencing is a by-product of the way in which the brain developed and is inter-connected, and no longer feel so shamed by 'unreasonable' emotions and a sense of individual pathology.

The research behind our understanding of the different types of memory has been reviewed, along with the way in which the phenomenon has been tackled in psychodynamic and CBT therapy. The role of the past in the difficulties experienced by our three case examples has then been added to what we know about them so far.

The role of emotion has underpinned much of this discussion, as it is the emotion, with accompanying physical mobilization, that is transported from distant trauma into the midst of the current crisis by the emotional memory, acting in ignorance of time and context. The positive use of emotion as the central means to heal that disrupted relationship with the past has been introduced. It is to consideration of emotion, both in its potential for distress and destabilization, and for healing and resolution, that we now turn, in the next chapter.

Section II

Opportunity, emotions and the elusive self

Emotions manage relationship and the self is a relationship (with itself) so that the themes of this section are intertwined.

DOI: 10.4324/9781003081616-7

Section II

Opportunity, emotions and the elusive self

6 Emotion as problem, emotion as solution

Introductory summary

This chapter outlines the pervasiveness of a dysfunctional relationship with emotions. This affects individuals; all individuals, not just those with identified mental health problems, and it affects society as a whole. Facing reality requires facing the emotion that goes with that. This is not the prevailing stance – emotions are to be avoided, fixed or offloaded onto somebody else (whose fault is it: who do we sue?). Chronic avoidance of emotion lies at the heart of addiction, and it can be argued that society is riven with addictions, whether to consumerism, celebrity culture or drink and drugs. Such addictions assist with not facing a challenging reality. However, where emotions can be faced, expressed healthily and let go of, they can smooth the way to facing that reality, applying intelligence to whatever can be solved, and bearing the pain of what needs to be accepted. This is relevant both at a societal and an individual level, and this section will start to address the impact of both these levels of adversity on the individual.

Emotions are here viewed as a conduit to a new adaptation. Where the old way has led to an impasse, a new way through is needed. Grief and tears facilitate coming to terms with unbearable loss, making moving forward possible. Anger holds within itself energy for change and the sense of having a right, which can provide the courage and motivation necessary to face daunting challenges and to make the most of potential – and so on for other emotions.

The role of emotion

Both Tasha and Kath came into the services with complaints that can be traced straightforwardly to wayward emotions. For Tasha, these interfered with her concentration on her studies and led to serious self-harm. Kath's despair and sadness (depression) has been with her for years, with extra stress and anger more recently joining the mix. In Raju's case, the role of emotions, other than anger at Ambika's attempts to help, are less evident. However, the stresses of being caught between the expectations of his family and his failure at a job he never wanted, which contrasts with his wife's success, are evident, and could well be driving him away from consensual reality towards a world that is less punishing and more rewarding.

DOI: 10.4324/9781003081616-8

Referring back to the States of Mind diagram (Figure 1.1) enables us to understand the mechanism whereby, for each of these three, their situation has become intolerable. Where stresses multiply and increase, the emotion mind or implicational subsystem becomes dominant. The body is recruited to meet the threat. It is either shut down to avoid unequal competition as in depression, or got ready for immediate action; fight or flight – except that physical action is not appropriate or helpful here. The emotion mind takeover leads to narrowing focus into tunnel vision and losing the ability to draw on the wider perspective offered by the reasonable mind or propositional subsystem. Also, loss of access to the propositional means that the vivid memory for past threat, held in the implicational memory, holds sway, unchecked by the sense that that was all a long time ago and it is different now.

In Raju's case, the two central subsystems have got sufficiently out of line that he is losing touch with his reasonable mind altogether. Given the situation he finds himself in, it is possible to sympathize with not wanting to face its reality. The same could be said for the other two, and though retreating into depression and resorting to self-harm are less drastic strategies than shifting into another dimension, all are responses to intolerable and apparently unresolvable life circumstances, intensified by resonances from the past.

All three examples involve the role of conflicted and problematic relationships, both in the past and in the present. This illustrates the close link between emotion and relationship, which is not surprising if it is accepted that the role of emotion is the regulation of relationship. In Kath's case, she went from a difficult relationship with her father to an abusive one with her husband, followed more recently by an even worse relationship that she is now trying to escape from. This has also spilled out into fraught relations at work, not helped by her concern for the plight of her mother. Tasha has been subjected to the frightening, damaging and confusing experience of prolonged childhood sexual abuse accompanied by threats. This has complicated her relationship with her mother; her relationship with her brother is similarly ambiguous. We do not yet know why things have come to a head now. Raju is torn between his family of origin, his marriage and his inability to be true to himself, because of the unsuitable career he has been forced to pursue.

Raju's example here introduces another important relationship; the relationship between the individual and themselves. In common with practically everyone who comes into contact with the mental health services, this self/self-relationship is not good. Kath puts herself down when depressed. Tasha physically attacks herself. Raju is forced into a situation where he must suppress his very real talents and potential. There is probably an element of suppressed potential present for all three. Tasha is not putting all her energy into studies which could promise a good career. Kath is valued at work, but her mental health difficulties are undermining her attendance and hence, her position.

Coping with emotions and relationships – the bigger picture

Our example cases are not alone in struggling with emotions and relationships. As remarked in Chapter 1, literature, films and stories would be unrecognizable if managing emotions and relationships was always straightforward and controllable. A question I always ask when delivering training in this model is: 'How do we as a society, and as a health service, deal with emotions?' I write this book in the early weeks of the country grappling with COVID-19, and the fears and restrictions this brings with it. Some people are reacting to the crisis by buying up everything they can lay their hands on, whereas others are showing great altruism and self-sacrifice, not least the front-line health professionals. However, before the world as we knew it was consigned to history, the more general media and public reaction to adverse events was either: 'Whose fault is it? Who do we sue?' or denial and distraction: 'It isn't that bad really' (in defiance of facts), or 'Have a drink; go to the doctor and get some tablets, etc.'. There seems to be a denial of the ultimate inevitability of death in the expectation of a medical solution to essentially fatal illness, especially (understandably) when such illness affects young children. The same mind-set leads to the expectation that mental health services should be able to prevent every suicide.

Maybe our particular Western society, as a whole, struggles with painful emotions by trying to side-line them. In Chapter 4, I argued that we are all bound up in a web of relationships; that, where our implicational mode of being is dominant, we essentially are relationship, and that the character of those relationships affects us to the core of our being. Where they are loving and nurturing, we will feel safe and happy, and that could be the case for the relationships over which we have most immediate control; those with our friends and family. However, in the case of the wider relationships, with other groups of people on the planet whose situation is less secure for instance, or with the earth itself, the situation is less positive. One particular example is the growing recognition that the foundations of modern capitalism are inextricably bound up with an exploitative and in some cases exterminative colonial past. The descendants of the exploiters and the exploited are now mingled in our society, and the unease of that situation, as well as the legacy of past wrongs (as past and present are the same in this relational mode of being) create the pervasive evil of racism, on a continuum that runs from unease to overt violence, with all possible stages in between.

This involuntary involvement with dysfunctional relationships leaves an underlying emotional residue, registered at the level of felt sense, but mostly unrecognized and unacknowledged. As with most implicational phenomena, this hypothesis cannot be pinned down with hard facts, as that sort of evidence is the province of the other way of knowing. All we can do is to take readings of what is probably a pervasive and accepted emotional tone of unease, and speculate. It could be that this unease contributes to the need to pacify the internal felt sense with things that distract or numb, whether these are the obvious fuels for addiction, such as alcohol, drugs, gambling or the softer go-tos such as junk food, shopping and entertainment.

Of course, this argument needs nuancing. There is balance here. As remarked earlier, things that can be life enhancing (e.g. the arts, entertainment, travel), can equally be used in a way that is numbing (wall to wall vapid TV, compulsive computer game playing, 'consumption' of exotic locations) and the same goes for the whole list. However, it is an economy based on reckless consumption that only works if constantly buying new things and dashing to new places is the norm, which is destroying the planet. These observations extend beyond the scope of this book, except that recognizing the extent to which we are all tangled into what could be seen as a dysfunctional system, with impact on our emotional life and how we manage it, can help in breaking down the 'them and us' barrier between those who experience mental breakdown and those who manage to maintain mental balance, however precariously.

To return to the topic of emotions and mental breakdown, a medically oriented mental health service will expect to find a solution, a fix, for whatever is presented, as that is what doctors do: cure people; take away their symptoms. However, if the argument is accepted, that mental health issues are to do with out-of-control feelings, in reaction to real experiences and relationships, both past and present, there isn't an easy fix or cure. How do we give Tasha back the childhood she should have had? How do we stop Kath sinking into periodic despair and prevent her ex-boyfriend from harassing her? How do we disentangle Raju from the expectations of others so that he can live the life that would work for him? Medication is hardly the solution here, and there might not be a total solution, only amelioration. Once we stop trying to side-line or deny emotions, we might just be able to use them to improve matters.

The positive potential of emotion

Emotions have an important function. As well as managing relationships, they are constituted to look after the self; to keep us safe from both physical and social danger, and enable us to operate effectively in the world. Once you stop running away from emotions, it becomes possible to understand how they work, and how they might be part of the solution. DBT has a good way of conceptualizing an emotion (Linehan 1993, p. 87) An emotion is compared to a wave. Left to itself, it has a natural course, which is time limited. However, it is easy to interfere with that natural course in such a way as to keep the emotion around and prevent it dying away in accordance with its own rhythm. Anxiety and anger are simple examples here. Both emotions connect directly with the body's fight/flight adrenalin driven pathway; in other words, they mobilize the body for action, and trigger parallel changes in brain chemistry. DBT teaches mindfulness to observe this phenomenon, with detached curiosity, and let it take its course. This mindful detachment ensures that the reasonable mind, or propositional subsystem becomes accessible once more, so that, to use DBT terminology, a 'Wise Mind' course of action can be decided upon.

However, this is not the usual course of things! Faced with fear, the natural reaction is to flinch, to try to avoid or block it out. In this way, the emotion is not allowed to run its natural course. Then the mind comes in and rehearses anxious thoughts – rumination – which keep the anxiety present, along with the physical stress reaction. In the case of anger, the process can be similar – avoidance and rumination, or the impulse to act might be carried through in words or gestures. Again, ruminating on the slight, or whatever, will keep that emotion on the boil, and the body in a state of readiness for action: in other words, stress. Attempting to suppress anger will only allow it to build in the background, and perhaps break out in disproportionate reaction to something relatively trivial. All this enables the emotion to stick around and hold sway, assisted by the emotion mind, implicational, memory 'helpfully' adding past hurts or terrors to the mix. Other emotions, such as guilt, shame and sadness operate in a similar manner. Guilt and shame are particularly sticky and difficult to send upon their way.

So, it is easy to mess up an emotion and ensure that it keeps you tangled up with an unpleasant internal state, high stress and unhelpful impulses to action. On the other hand, by facing the emotion and expressing it in a sound way, even the 'negative' emotions can become allies. Take the sadness that inevitably follows loss. That has the potential to become bogged down in ruminative thinking which will keep it around forever. But, as human beings, we have been given the gift of tears to enable us to meet and express that grief. Those tears, and the facial expression and bodily demeanour that goes with them, will communicate directly with others, who will be moved to share the grief and offer support, as emotions operate between people. Provided the tears are allowed their natural flow, and are followed by a turning to the continuing life in the present, this process will allow the natural healing of the breach in the very fabric of our being that major loss represents. This process can work for more complex losses – such as the loss of the good childhood (cf. Tasha), and so help with the vital work of healing and coming to terms with the past. This healing process can easily be short circuited if others signal that they cannot bear that depth of feeling by trying to cheer the individual up too quickly. This communicates 'Just don't go there', a message that is similarly implied when the individual or those around them look for blame and revenge as a way of avoiding the raw pain of grief.

All the emotions have this healing and life-giving potential, provided the immediate impulse to act on them can be halted, and the emotion and its triggers brought into the light of 'wise mind' – that place where the implicational and propositional subsystems are in good communication. In the case of fear, it is a matter of determining whether there actually is a present threat, and problem solving how to meet it. If it turns out the fear belongs to the past, or is out of proportion, reversing avoidance, exposure, at a manageable pace is the way to escape a situation where life is controlled and limited by the feeling. Disgust is another emotion that requires particularly careful exposure, as it is such a visceral experience and can easily overwhelm.

Guilt is a feeling that lends itself to unproductive rumination. Its adapted aspect is a call to take responsibility and possibly make repair for something. All too often, however, it is exaggerated and mired in the past, and needs repeated mindful letting go, and the sort of attention to the self/self-relationship to be discussed in the next chapter. Shame is another challenging emotion to manage in the light of wise mind. It somehow gnaws at the foundations of the self and is therefore acutely uncomfortable to face head on. All too easily, the natural flinch reaction to overwhelming emotional pain switches it into either anger or withdrawal, so that it remains unexamined. Again, self-compassion and acceptance of what is past are the route to repair.

The positive potential of anger

Anger is the emotion that has attracted the worst press, but actually has the greatest potential to turn things around – if properly managed. It has already been noted that the emotions have an important function to look after the self, and anger is given to us to be our primary protection. It is important to distinguish 'anger', the emotion, from 'violence', which is a behaviour. Emotions just arise in response to a trigger. No one can be blamed for having an emotion. Impulses to action, behaviours, can either be given into or inhibited. There is always a choice about whether to act or not.

The anger reaction signals that something is not right and needs addressing. This is important information, but where the immediate, violent and immoderate action that anger can trigger is feared, or prohibition of the expression of anger has been powerfully instilled through socialization, this vital learning can be buried, and the individual remains defenceless against harm and exploitation. Of course, the present anger response might be reinforced by, or mainly relevant to, threats way in the past, because of the way that the implicational memory operates outside of time. Only wise mind, the two central subsystems working in conjunction, can sort out what belongs to now and needs addressing, if practical, and what belongs to the past. As the impulse to action is particularly powerful in the case of anger, this needs a two-stage response; first facing the impulse – short-circuiting the natural flinch reaction that might bury it, and then taking charge of the body's call to action: buying time by leaving the situation temporarily; switching off action mode by long, slow outbreath breathing; counting to ten – whatever is practical in the situation.

Once wise mind has been restored by such means, it becomes possible to view the situation from a perspective of mindfulness, and a considered response, a choice, is possible. It must be emphasized that facing an unpalatable situation in wise mind is always challenging – whether it is the raw pain of grief, the complex wound to self of shame, or the perception of attack that leads to anger. This is why the flinch reaction is immediate and natural, and where it becomes habitual, it leads to the avoidance of emotion and all the ills that this entails. Some people, of course, do not flinch when faced with anger; they give in to it. This too is an avoidance of facing the situation. The adrenalin rush provides a buzz that takes the person through. It is only afterwards that they need to face the consequences of their reaction. Some people unfortunately learn to manage the complexities of life by giving into their anger. This apparently circumvents the need to learn how to negotiate relationships, as they can rely on others to fall in with their wishes through fear.

Once the anger situation can be appraised mindfully, choices can be made. Where the circumstances need addressing and can be addressed, problem solving comes into play. Where the situation is not amenable to action, or action would be too costly (the government; your employer; the benefit system) or the real anger is about the past, the immediate rush to action needs discharging in some physical or creative manner. However, the original impulse should not be lost sight of. Anger about an unjust, abusive past (or present) is the clue to a sense of 'I had a right to better'. This is a strength. In Chapter 13, we will look in more detail at how this strength can be applied to provide the courage needed to work for radical change. Anger is often buried in other emotions, like depression and fear, and if uncovered and used wisely can provide the way forward. Fear and depression can paralyze, and that paralysis is often intensified where there is buried anger. Because anger provokes such a powerful mobilization of the body to action, it can provide the energy and motivation needed to pursue a new and challenging direction in life, provided it is liberated safely.

Conclusion and summary

This chapter has considered the powerful role of emotions, both within the individual and in the wider society. Again and again, the role of mindfulness, or bringing wise mind into play (which is the same thing) has been introduced. The common mistake is to see emotions as a problem to be disposed of – especially in the case of anger. Not only does this cut off their potential for fostering growth and healing, it also denies our very humanity. In the same way that a plant needs light, soil, water and space to grow, human beings need to be able to meet, accept and flex their emotions in order to manage the challenges that life inevitably brings, and to realize their full potential.

However, emotions can be uncomfortable, both for the person experiencing them and for those around. Emotions operate in the space between people, managing the relationship between people, whether affiliative or hostile. Further, their vital connection with the body and the mobilization of its immediate action system can make them dangerous, as action without due thought and consideration of the wider context is frequently disastrous. Courage and resilience are needed in order to bear the pain attendant on living. Emotions offer both, provided we are in right relationship with them.

This section of the book will expand on how the CCC approach to emotions is about building a right relationship with them, and meeting the challenges they bring. Their rhythm and mode of operation must be respected, but they also need to be brought into line with reasonable mind reality. As well as unhitching from the impulse to immediate action, they need space for expression. This applies to all emotions, and the tendency to sort them into 'positive' and 'negative' is to be resisted. They all have their role and need respect.

This stance runs counter to much that is accepted as the norm in our society. The illness model tends to see 'negative' emotions such as sadness and fear as 'symptoms' (depression and anxiety) to be eliminated, whether through medication or targeted therapy. While undoubtedly excessive fear, sadness and anger can overwhelm life and become a problem, the CCC approach is to allow the emotions to flow through and therefore not stick around and take over. This contrasts with an expectation of becoming free of emotions. For many people, periodic return of strong emotion is a part of their life and who they are. Kath's recurrent depression is an example here. The answer in such cases is to accept and learn to live with the down (or the up) times, aware that, if properly managed, they will pass.

Having considered the relationship with the emotions, the next chapter will go on to examine the relationship both with and within the self. This taps into a core theme, already touched upon, which recurs within CCC, of the multiple, shifting sands, nature of the self.

7 The elusive self

Compassion and potential

Introductory summary

The idea of the self as 'work in progress' has been introduced in Chapter 1. This idea is developed further here. The relationship between an individual and themselves is the starting point. Often, particularly in the case of mental health problems, this lies at the heart of the problem. We are taught to expect others to look after our emotional needs, but in our fragmented society, that often just does not happen. The only solution is to apply the necessary compassion to ourselves, which might be the last thing that comes naturally. This chapter examines the background to our understanding of the self/self-relationship and how it can be developed within therapy at the implicational/felt sense level; the only one that is likely to be effective.

Next, the multiplicity of the self is considered. The idea that 'our selves' are constituted of varied aspects, reflected in different roles and moods, is presented along with their origin in relationships. The phenomenon of dissociation, which can create gulfs between the different aspects, arising when emotions are unbearable, is discussed. The idea that the individual can develop an awareness of this process and steer it is introduced. This can involve, for instance, noting and perhaps curbing a dominant aspect which tends to take over and presume to speak for the whole, or bringing forward undeveloped aspects and allowing them space. This insight into the self and its fluidity allows room for growth and development. Mindfulness is offered as the means to aid this process, while recognizing that with no overall control, no boss self, total mastery is an illusion.

'The self' dethroned

The ICS conclusion that 'there is no boss' dethrones the notion of a 'self' that is in charge, and replaces it with a process of shifting control, handing the baton back and forth between the implicational and propositional (emotional and reasonable) networks in the brain in a way which is often smooth, but can become disrupted, resulting in the implicational gaining greater dominance. This happens at low arousal; when we switch off the apparatus to sleep, or let it coast, and at high arousal, when the implicational picks up potential threat to the self. Even when we

DOI: 10.4324/9781003081616-9

are conducting our lives with a good exchange between the two, the implicational is always lurking somewhere in the background, ready to take charge when matters pertaining to the safety or status of the self arise. With a hotline to the body, this might mean that it launches into action, leaving the propositional to come up with a plausible story about what has occurred, endeavouring to show the individual in the best light in the circumstances, for the outer world's consumption. We experience this take-over subjectively in our felt sense, our gut feeling, that tells us when things are not right.

This fluid process means that our sense of self, of who we are, is built up from a sum of experiences. Where and how we sit within our web of connection, and the history to that, is the bedrock. However, built on that bedrock are the habitual ways we learn to manage things, which determines our 'self' in real time. This has implications. It means that we cannot take our 'self' for granted, but it also means that by deciding to manage things differently, to cope in a new way, we can exercise more control over the process.

Recognizing the web of connection as a bedrock founds the whole edifice on relationship. The obvious relationships are with people outside of us. This chapter shines the spotlight on another world of relationship; the relationships within ourselves. The relationship that each one of us has with our own self is crucial. The nature of this relationship is revealed in how we treat ourselves, how we talk to ourselves through the internal dialogue. The other vital internal relationship is between the different aspects and potentials of our self, varying according to our different roles, relationships and moods, each one with history linking to our individual past.

So, 'the self' is not a given, but rather a dynamic, fluctuating, system, drawing information moment by moment, which is registered in felt sense, and accumulates a way of navigating the world over time. This way of operating is reflected in stable patterns of relationship. The system is in turn built on the foundation of earlier experiences of relating which have been internalized, as discussed in Chapter 4. This is not necessarily a particularly solid or sound foundation, as we have seen in the discussion of the effects of trauma in Chapter 5. The relationship that is in every sense closest to home is the relationship each one of us has with our own self. The wider social and relational context might be largely beyond our control, but the self/self-relationship is one that we can work to improve – but before that can occur we need to become aware that we have one.

The self/self-relationship

In Chapter 3, we introduced the idea that healing the self/self-relationship lies at the heart of the enterprise of therapy because of the way mental health difficulties manifest themselves through this relationship. For instance, when experiencing depression, Kath stopped looking after herself, became highly self-critical, while ceasing to maintain necessary routine, including work, and Tasha goes further in actually attacking herself, sometimes to a dangerous extent. Other people plan to kill themselves, and some succeed; others still restrict food, or engage in lifestyles, such as drug abuse, that are not conducive to health and self-preservation. If challenged as to whether they would treat a friend in the manner they are treating themselves, the answer is normally a horrified: 'No!'

Becoming aware of what is going on, through a simple practice of mindfulness, is basic for CCC, and this can put the internal dialogue, that conversation that is the normal vehicle for thought, in the spotlight. The internal dialogue, which usually rumbles on unobserved in the background, reveals the nature of the self/ self-relationship. For example, Kath's CBT enabled her to spot her self-critical negative automatic thoughts (NATs, in CBT speak), but she found it hard to challenge them when she was depressed, even when it was pointed out to her that she would never say those things to a friend. At such times, they just felt 'right'. Her reasonable mind (propositional subsystem) could see that they were not necessarily logically justified, but when depression engulfed her, emotion mind took over and that perspective went out the window. It is therefore essential to tackle these thoughts at the emotion mind, implicational, level.

There are three stages to this. The first, awareness of the nature of the internal dialogue or NATs, has been covered. The second is to bring to life the concept of relationship, so that impact of a bullying and of a nurturing relationship is experienced imaginatively at the implicational level, along with awareness that we are here dealing with a real relationship, but within the individual. The third stage brings in advances made in Compassion Focused Therapy (CFT), in both understanding how compassionate relationships work and in promoting self-compassion (Gilbert 2005).

To summarize CFT, Gilbert identifies two states within the emotional mind: threat, and soothing/safeness. The soothing/safeness state has the power to de-activate the threat state. Accessing one or other state is dependent on relationship – both current and historical. This distinction is based on polyvagal theory (Porges 2009, Dana 2018), which refines our understanding of the workings of the sympathetic (stress reaction system) and parasympathetic nervous systems. The vagus nerve that carries messages for the parasympathetic system has two pathways. Where safety in the context of relationship is experienced, this cues closeness and warmth, which in turn is calming and soothing to the whole system. In contrast, where danger is sensed, that closeness is shut off through a freeze response. All mammals need this system as their social and parental systems are built on mutual support and literal huddling together. They also need to know when it is not safe to make themselves vulnerable in this way. For human beings, this basic freeze response can translate into the dissociation we have noted as a defence in the face of trauma in Chapter 5.

Gilbert argues, on the basis of research into neurobiology (e.g. Depue & Morrone-Strupinsky 2005), that our minds have evolved to co-regulate each other in this way. Just as a threatening relationship will trigger adrenalin release to activate the threat system, signals of safeness and soothing will release oxytocin and endorphins. So, to be effective, the self-compassionate relationship needs to be experienced at the felt sense level in order to release the relevant hormones. How this is managed within the programme, using mindfulness of self-compassion, will be covered in Chapter 14. Taking hold of and steering the self/self-relationship in this way can be a powerful intervention in service of breaking the vicious cycles that lie at the heart of mental health issues.

Aspects of self

This section will unpack the ICS based claim that the self is a work in progress and shifting sands, and will introduce the way in which CCC uses this to steer development in a sound direction and unlock under-expressed potential. To recap from Chapter 4, the sense of self is built up out of a patchwork of internalized relationships. We can modify how they are played out in our lives as we go along, or they can continue to control our actions and relationships undetected. The way in which important relationships, for instance with early caregivers, can be re-enacted within current relationships was noted by Freud and the early psychoanalysts, and known as 'transference'. These authors further recognized that the therapist was a human being too, with a similarly constituted self, so that the therapist's immediate reaction to these enactments was influenced by their own internalized relationships. This was labelled 'counter-transference'. The idea was that the insight the therapist had gained into their own internal world, through having themselves undergone analysis, would enable them to disentangle their own process from whatever the client was bringing, and so use the relationship in the present to modify, and free from the past, the client's mode of relating.

In CCC, the aim is to expand the client's ability to reflect on what is happening in the present through mindfulness, and so develop the ability to put the past in the past. The therapist will help them to develop this faculty, and model a compassionate, validating relationship, that is at the same time leading them forward to substitute sound coping for dysfunctional coping, in the interests of growth and the realization of potential.

Fluctuating experiences of the self are not confined to the therapy situation. Everyone can identify the phenomenon of 'being' different in different relational contexts. It is a strange human being who behaves in exactly the same way on a Saturday night out with good friends as they do on Monday morning at work. Most of us have one mode of relating when we are with our children, which needs to change as they grow up, and another of relating to our parents – which might reverse, as our parents age, and we become in turn more parental towards them, and so on. We might note that the way we relate to our children has echoes of how we were parented, representing expression of our internalization of that role; or we might consciously try to change the script, where we feel our own experience was less than optimal. In this way, the various aspects of ourselves, with their different potential for relating, are themselves forever in flux. They might be played out unreflectingly, or they might be consciously steered in a particular direction. The reader is here invited to reflect for themselves on the different 'aspects' that their varied roles and contexts can reveal.

As if being constituted from a patchwork of partially digested earlier relationships, along with adapting to an array of varied roles and contexts, were not enough to undermine the sense of a stable and unitary self, there is the capacity of emotion mind (implicational) to take over and inject further chaos. As we have seen in the previous chapter, our emotional mind has the power to hijack the way we are operating in the world and yank us off in a direction that later cool reflection regrets. This occurs, for instance, when the threat system is activated; fear or anger take over, and we discover that we have either avoided something we should have faced up to, or resorted to unfortunate words or actions. In this way, our different moods provide the basis for yet more possible and distinct aspects of ourselves, often linking with the aspects that arise out of roles and relationships.

These shifting components of self mean that gaining a sense of 'who we are' cannot be taken for granted. This 'work in progress' is particularly evident in adolescence, when the work of building and discovering the self is most active and urgent. Traditionally, this was undertaken via relationships (those intense friendships and love affairs), bolstered by admiration from afar; crushes and heroes. These larger-than-life figures provide a comparison and an ideal to aim at in the process of creating a self. Social media has now put that whole process on steroids, with instant approval or demolition available at the click of a mouse. By contrast, in more stable societies than ours, where people's life path was mapped out for them by others, these pressures will have been far less (for some, of course, this will have resulted in thwarted potential).

Though the process of making your 'self' slows in adulthood, it never ceases throughout life. The extraordinary potency, both social and financial, of celebrities, whether in the arts, sport or simply influencers, bears witness to this. People need such reference points in order to find out who they are. They can then try out their current version of themselves in social or work situations, or over social media, and how they feel inside will be greatly impacted by the perceived (because their estimation of this can be biased in either a positive or a negative direction) response. This is what I mean by the elusive self.

Appreciating the universal background effort to attain and maintain this adequate experience of self allows us to see mental health in a new light. The delicate balance of achieving a 'good enough' internal state is revealed. For many, this has to be pursued in the face of overwhelming odds, whether the result of past experience or current context. The wonder is not so much that this balance falters, but that so many of us stay upright while navigating these shifting sands.

Therapy and the multiple self

There are a number of ways of approaching the phenomenon of different aspects of self among the various schools of therapy. Reciprocal roles and self-states in CAT; part objects in Object Relations theory; schemas and modes within CBT, and the more recent vogue for 'chair work' all capture this same facet of human experience. My therapeutic practice has been influenced by the humanistic conceptualization of 'subpersonalities' (Rowan 1990). Subpersonality work brings the topic to life, which is effective for implicational level working (chair work has a similar effect). I prefer the label 'aspect of self' to 'subpersonality', as it somehow seems to allow for more fluidity, the feature I want to emphasize.

Greater fluidity between the different aspects is a mark of good mental health. Problems arise when the person finds themselves stuck with a diminished array, or when their various aspects are too sharply separated from each other. This occurs where the developmental process has been disrupted through extreme threat, leading to dissociation. Dissociation is a natural defensive mechanism, triggered by repeated and prolonged threatening and abusive experiences from a young age. Dissociation can remove the individual mentally from situations that they cannot escape physically, but which are unbearable, and also destructive to their sense of self. Sexual abuse from a family member is an example of an experience that cannot be incorporated into a good sense of self. The child must rely on their caregiver for survival, yet they are being violated by the person they need to trust. In the face of such irreconcilable internal conflict, switching off is the safest solution.

Such dissociation interferes with the ability of the propositional to make links with the implicational, so that the different experiences of the self in different circumstances remain cut off, and the adult can find themselves switching involuntarily from one to another, usually in response to something that threatens to trigger an unbearable memory. Such a switch can facilitate escape from a 'no-go' zone within the self. In extreme forms, the different aspects can appear to be unaware of each other, and this has attracted the label of Dissociative Identity Disorder or DID. See Kennedy, Kennerley & Pearson 2013 for a thorough treatment of dissociation.

While dissociation can cause someone to jump between aspects, a more common problem is becoming imprisoned in an impoverished subset of the potentially available aspects. Being gripped by emotions like fear and helplessness can trap someone in a limited repertoire of behaviours, and cause them to abandon or lose sight of their wider horizons. Kath finds it too much even to keep work going when depressed, let alone engage in whatever else might make life more meaningful; Tasha allows her studies to slip, and Raju has become locked in an unreal world, divorced from the potential offered by his marriage, family and professional life.

With everyone, a particular aspect will be the dominant one at a particular time, in response to the situation. Thus, I might inhabit my professional self at work and then transition to another aspect at the end of the day. The aspect in charge in the moment will, at that time, 'feel' like 'me'. Where the self-system becomes stuck, that sense can feel absolute, and the current aspect speaks authoritatively for the whole. This can be dangerous, as we can see in Raju's case, or in Kath's when everything seems hopeless for ever, so there is no point in making an effort. In this situation, the individual needs to become aware of the other potentials and the possibility to move towards them.

The other danger is that a particular potential is labelled as 'the villain' and efforts are made to squash it. It is important to look for the positive in even apparently destructive aspects. Features such as dogged self-preservation or determination that can be present in 'negative' aspects have the potential to be helpful when disengaged from damaging behaviours, whereas disowning parts of oneself is never a good idea.

Similarly, aspects that someone might want to promote as 'myself', such as conscientious perfectionism, invariably turn out to have a flip side if allowed too much leeway. The way to health is an ability to move between aspects, bringing out the best in each, and giving oxygen to undeveloped potential. A mindful observing capacity is necessary for this, and an ability to tolerate uncertainty and imperfection. This is challenging for many people, particularly where their threat systems are well developed with good reason. Fear and exploration do not go naturally together.

CCC has developed a specific approach to using this multiplicity of the self in the interests of escaping from stuck places and promoting growth and development of the self, which will be discussed in Chapter 16. Seeing the self as work in progress means that there is room for this growth and development, and for consciously leaving behind discouraging messages about the self received in the past. This is an optimistic therapeutic approach with more emphasis on potential than pathology.

Conclusion and summary

This chapter has attempted an exploration of the complex tangle that is the human self through consideration of internal relationships; both the relationship we all have with ourselves, expressed through the internal dialogue, and the relationship between the different parts of the self. Mindfulness is the common means to eavesdrop on that internal dialogue, and so uncover the nature of the self/self-relationship, and to navigate between the different aspects, actualized and potential, that make up the self. Bringing the mind into a state of observing awareness both enables us find out what is going on at this, normally subterranean, level of the self, and to intervene and steer where advisable. Mental health breakdown will signal that this level of internal relationship is malfunctioning in some way. Maybe the self/self-relationship has become toxic, attacking or neglectful. Maybe one part of the self has taken over and excluded the others, resulting in the person being less than they might be. If it is a dangerous part, for instance one that sees suicide as the solution, the whole of that individual is endangered. However, recognizing that one part is purporting to speak for the whole offers a way forward in this perilous situation.

The next chapter explores a further potential of this distributed model of the self by uncovering what may be going on when we move beyond our groundedness in individual self-consciousness. This perspective offers a new insight into those experiences that take human beings away from the safe limitations of ordinary consciousness into places that can be ecstatic, or terrifying; earnestly pursued or greatly to be feared. Language is treacherous here. Immediately we label this area of experience as either spiritual or psychotic, we consign it to opposite ends of a spectrum. Once we learn to see the human being as scattered between relationships, both internal and external, both past and present, it becomes possible to collapse that spectrum and view this feared and fascinating dimension of experience as one. The task is then to learn to manage it, to cope, in ways that are life enhancing and not diminishing.

8 Beyond consensual reality

Introductory summary

The idea, first introduced in Chapter 4, that human beings encounter the world through two distinct ways of knowing, is picked up and explored more fully here. The human potential for anomalous experiencing is linked to the ICS model of brain organization. The dominance of the 'normal', scientific, way of knowing, is noted and its limitations are explored. The extent to which it is complemented by the experiential way of knowing is revealed and this is linked to the central place given to felt sense within CCC.

This leads onto exploration of the further limits of the experiential way of knowing, where it strays beyond the boundaries of the individual self and flows into the 'transliminal', introduced first in Chapter 4. The characteristics of the transliminal are expounded, including its numinosity, synchronicities, the dissolution of boundaries between self and other, and the implications for the self. The logic governing this other, transliminal, way of knowing is discussed, along with the limitations this represents for human knowledge.

Taking experience seriously

For those who have followed the argument of the book thus far, any notion of a simple, unitary self has hopefully been thoroughly deconstructed. It is now time for more in-depth exploration of how we know about the world. Chapter 1 invited re-examination of key assumptions, looking for the untidy gaps and edges in the accepted story. The notion of two distinct ways in which our sensory and information processing apparatus gives us access to the world out there, constitutes one such gap; it means that, as human beings, we have two different, and not necessarily compatible ways of knowing. Now it is time to develop this idea and to ground it in ICS insights into brain wiring, first revisiting these two ways of knowing and what they are like.

The first is the one we take for granted; ordinary, focused, waking consciousness, which enables us to pin down physical reality and make reliable predictions. This is the realm that science operates in, but even science has discovered, since the 20th century, that it only operates in this predictable way within a limited context,

DOI: 10.4324/9781003081616-10

and the very large and the very small lie outside that range, hence the paradoxical findings of Quantum Theory. However, that is a special case, and for everyday life, this way of knowing introduces a comforting degree of predictability.

As we have seen in Chapter 4, the other way of knowing is encountered in its more extreme form in altered states of consciousness, whether sought through taking substances or engaging in certain practices; or maybe stumbled upon, as in the case of a spontaneous spiritual experience or psychotic episode (more on that later). However, it is also involved in appreciation of art, beauty, relationship, emotion – everything that adds colour to the experience of being human. By privileging felt sense, CCC takes this way of knowing very seriously.

As already discussed, which way of knowing is dominant depends on whether the two main subsystems, propositional and implicational, are working smoothly together, or whether the implicational (emotional) subsystem has become dominant. Because our minds are designed to smooth over discontinuities and come up with a consistent story, we are normally unaware of this process. This smoothing over feature of our information processing can be seen most clearly in the way visual perception works, but holds across the board. Further, where we do hit incompatibilities, in our culture we invariably favour the 'scientific' way of knowing, achieved when the two main subsystems are working together. As a result we generally find a way to side-line information picked up by the other, experiential, way of knowing that doesn't fit in. Parapsychology is a good example here. It is subjected to scientific scrutiny and proves slippery, but enough solid evidence remains, along with conviction based on experience, that parapsychological phenomenon are 'real' among too many people to make it easy to dismiss out of hand. A different tactic is employed in the case of religion, another area fundamentally dependent on experiential knowing and shy of scientific verification. Religion is broadly tolerated as a special case; a phenomenon to be accepted (and possibly ignored) without too much scrutiny.

A lot of the time, sticking with the scientific way of knowing serves us well. Our scientific and technologically driven society is built upon that bias. However, marginalizing the information that somehow manages to by-pass the propositional and comes directly from experience, where it does not fit in neatly with the agreed picture, leaves us impoverished in certain areas, and understanding mental health is one of these. As the argument of this book is that mental health problems have their origin in managing felt sense, and therefore, experience, this is territory we need to explore.

A central issue here is the failure to recognize the existence of experience as a distinct way of knowing. As covered in Chapter 4, the only way we can 'know' about relationship is experientially, and judgements about who we should avoid and who commit our lives to are surely among the most important that any one of us has to make. The whole gamut of the arts, including music, comes into this category, as well as areas such as sport (and dance) which are only experienced at their truest peak through directly relating to the body, cutting out the thinking mind – though this needs to be involved, particularly in the training process.

Experience beyond the self

Disengaging the busy, thinking mind (propositional and implicational working together) is an experience that is recognized and valued in all ages and societies: getting into 'the zone'; giving oneself up to rhythm, sound and music, along with other experiences such as sex, the contemplation of beauty, and indeed, mind altering substances, have the facility to enable the individual to step beyond 'themselves'; beyond the busy, self-conscious, individual, mind. This phenomenon has already been noted in Chapter 4 as stepping into a place of relatedness. Crowd experiences have this effect – the euphoria of the football crowd or large demonstration (and size is significant here; there is something about more-than-human scale that can transport us in this way – the medieval cathedral builders knew what they were doing). Everything listed here is a commonplace of human life, but not recognized as the opening into another way of experiencing, which can be encountered in a mild form (a lingering kiss, a beautiful picture or sunset) moving through more powerful expressions – ecstatic dance, transporting music – to a place that is truly beyond the self; the mystical or the psychotic experience. The word 'transliminal', or 'beyond the threshold', has been introduced to pin down this crucial but widely unrecognized concept.

I first became interested in getting to grips with this area of experience when I studied psychology in mid-life in order to effect a career change. I wanted to see what psychology could achieve in explaining the phenomenon of spirituality, which had been a lifelong interest of mine, and probably influenced my previous choice of subject to study: medieval history. Having failed to find much of use in the extant literature, I explored for myself, and concluded that spirituality represented a stepping outside of the construction of experience created by our thinking minds, a conceptualization based on Kelly's Construct Theory (Bannister & Fransella 1971). Once I had trained as a Clinical Psychologist, I started working as a therapist in a psychiatric rehabilitation service and was seeing people lumbered with an, often decades long, diagnosis of schizophrenia. I recognized in their stories of early breakdown, regularities of experience found in the accounts of mystical experience left by the medieval saints I had studied in my earlier career. I realized that something fundamental and universal was going on, and it was at precisely this point that ICS was published, and a scientific framework for what I was grappling with presented itself: one that penetrated more deeply into cognitive science and brain architecture than Kelly's Constructs.

Phil Barnard, whose computer modelling of pathways in the brain is the foundation for ICS, wrote about the way that schizophrenia can be understood as a desynchrony between the propositional and implicational subsystems (Barnard 2003). I am here arguing that so-called 'schizophrenia' is just one manifestation of this sort of desynchrony, which in fact penetrates all facets of human life. We have already seen the impact that implicational dominance can have in plunging us into emotion mind, where feelings take over and logic goes out the window. In the case of accessing the transliminal – that area of experiencing across the threshold which can open us to both valued and feared experiences, the two meaning

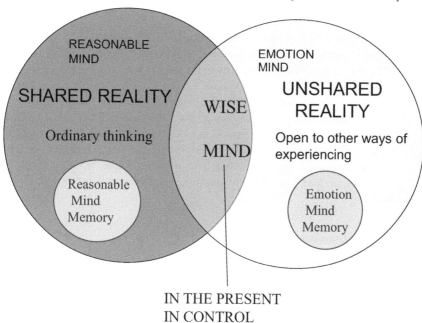

Figure 8.1 Shared and Unshared Reality

making systems have drifted further apart and the implicational has more truly taken over.

This can be illustrated by means of a modification of Figure 1.1, the diagram that presented Emotion Mind and Reasonable Mind with their associated memory systems, as follows. 'Shared' and 'Unshared Reality' are the terms I use to describe the states when working clinically.

The nature of these experiences, and their associated gains and losses, will be explored next.

The character of transliminal experience

Crossing that threshold into the transliminal means loss of the filter that normally constrains our experience. This filter enables us to focus in on detail and divide things up. Logic, sorting out what is and is not compatible, is at the heart of this faculty which becomes possible because we have a propositional subsystem and it connects with our implicational subsystem. Working together, they render our world manageable, but limited. Once we step beyond those limits, the character of the experience changes. There are no hard and fast rules here, and everyone's experience can be a bit different. It is inherently unpredictable, so the characteristics of transliminal experience that follow represent frequently observed generalities.

Enhanced experiencing

There is no generally accepted word for this in English. The Jungian term 'numinosity' expresses it well, but is not in wide usage. 'Supernatural' covers its spookier aspects. The writer on mysticism, Rudolph Otto (1917/1958), explored the concept of 'The Holy' which captures its spiritual/religious side. This sort of freeing, peak (to use Maslow's word) experience, is valued by those who ingest psychedelic substances, and is encountered in spiritual practice and spiritual experience. Emotion can be experienced in heightened form, and everything can become suffused with a sense of portentous meaning. Then again, in line with the paradoxical nature of this area which will be considered below, emotion might be completely absent and cut off; all meaning and comprehensibility radically unreachable.

Dissolution of boundaries

Entering the transliminal entails stepping beyond individuality and into a place of connection and relationship (in the abstract – conducting a real time relationship requires propositional fine tuning). The boundaries of the self can appear to dissolve, which can lead to an ecstatic experience of oneness with God, Goddess, etc. or the universe. Beyond the reach of propositional discriminative naming, these become indistinguishable. Less pleasant is the experience of being invaded, of one's thoughts no longer being private – maybe broadcast to the world; or of thoughts coming from beyond the self – beamed in by a satellite, or heard spoken out loud. It was by considering precisely what was being experienced as reported in such terms by the people I encountered in the psychiatric rehabilitation service, and working out the common denominator between a variety of 'symptoms', that I came to appreciate the centrality of dissolution of boundaries. The fact that the same core experience, differently described, can be discerned in the unitive experience of the mystics is interesting.

As well as fading boundaries between people, boundaries between inner and outer can disappear. Thoughts are experienced as voices. Things previously 'there' in the mind's eye are seen in the world, and past trauma, until now safely secured behind a wall of forgetting, can overwhelm. All these phenomena explain why, though a brief glimpse into the transliminal can be an exciting and life enhancing experience, staying too long, or worse, getting stuck there, is anything but. Further, dissolution of boundaries entails a sense of 'skinlessness', or porosity, sometimes leading to openness to being invaded or taken over by another being. 'Possession' states are a familiar phenomenon in many traditions, as is exorcism of such beings or spirits. For instance, within Islam, the Koran recognizes Djinn that have the capacity to enter someone and take over.

Channelling, or receiving extended messages, whole books (and even series of books in the case of *Conversations with God*, Walsch 1995), from 'beyond', written down by an individual who has no foreknowledge of, or propositional engagement with, the content, is another well recognized phenomenon. Such channelling is common among religious scriptures: the Koran was dictated to Mohammed by God, and the angel told St John what to write in the Book of Revelation in the New Testament of the Christian Bible. Mediums in the Spiritualist Church and elsewhere channel messages from the dead. Ancestors are frequently implicated in accounts of both possession and channelling.

A number of other reported phenomena, such as past life regression and reincarnation, where people claim access to knowledge for which there is no obvious source, could be at least partially explained if it were acknowledged that minds in a state of desynchrony between the propositional and implicational (i.e. having accessed the transliminal) may be able to either tap into or be taken over by alien psychic content – which might or might not have its origin in an identifiable source. Research into distance viewing has established that a state of deep relaxation, where the propositional will be in the background, is a necessary pre-condition for success (Radin 2006).

Parapsychological phenomena, such as telepathy and thought transference at a distance, can also be understood in terms of this dissolution of boundaries between people. Violation of time and space goes along with this, as other constraining factors that are shed once the propositional is out of the way (as we saw in the case of implicational memory and trauma in Chapter 5). People who have acquired a diagnosis of psychosis often claim paranormal powers. However, such a diagnosis is often acquired because such experiences can lead to extreme fear and sense of unsafety; imagine not being secure in your own skin. More generally, they lead to people coming to conclusions that others do not share. It can be that ordinary boundaries and safety are no longer understood, for example, someone believing that they can fly if they jump off the top of a multi-story car park. Emotions become unhinged from their true origins, leading to risk behaviour, which results in restrictions being placed on individuals in this state. In my clinical work, I use the terms 'shared' and 'unshared' reality. These acknowledge the reality of the experience for the individual, while emphasizing that they have become out of step with everyone else.

All things are connected

Along with shedding the ability to make fine discriminations, by employing 'either/or' logic, comes an often uncanny and deeply meaningful sense of abounding connections – the synchronicities that Jung, who was particularly interested in this area, speaks of. Whereas the propositional and implicational working together separate things out, the implicational left to an extent to itself sticks them together. More often, connections, such as reading significance into car number plates, so meaningful to the individual, seem anything but to the rest of the world. In other words, they are unshared reality. On the other hand, great art and literature can come from accessing a source beyond individuality – the classical idea that poetic and other artistic creativity was sent by the Muses is a case in point, and profound spiritual and mystical experiences invariably carry this aura of deep, universal, meaning.

The fate of the self

We have already seen that 'the self' is a more precarious entity than is generally assumed, and never more so than when the transliminal holds sway. Common 'psychotic symptoms' illustrate this. Claiming to be Jesus, Mohammed, a reincarnation of the Buddha or a famous pop star is common in this context. So too is a sense of the self being lost, dead, non-existent or deeply worthless. These contrasts illustrate another transliminal theme – extremes. Balance and the happy medium are ingredients added by the propositional.

In the spiritual literature, visions and mystical experiences characteristically signal the call to an important mission. This is a recurring theme for the Old Testament prophets. A well-known example is Isaiah's vision of heaven and encounter with God, an experience that was both stunning and terrifying (a seraphim put a burning coal on his lips). God called him to be a prophet, asking 'Whom shall I send?' to which Isaiah replied in the affirmative (Isaiah 1, Chapter 6, v. 8).

The fate of the self, faced with the transliminal, is noted thus by William James (1902/1978): 'an immense elation and freedom, as the outlines of the confining selfhood melt down'. Laing (1967) writes:

> The 'ego' is the instrument for living in *this* world. If the 'ego' is broken up, or destroyed ... then the person may be exposed to other worlds, 'real' in different ways from the more familiar territory of dreams, imagination, perception or phantasy.

In ICS terms, the ego roughly equates to implicational and propositional in alliance.

Such instances give us the clue that the sense of a stable, self-conscious, self is an epiphenomenon of the implicational and propositional working together, that came about by the addition of the propositional in our evolutionary trajectory. It begins to be possible to see how powerful leaders, gurus and celebrities tap into this transliminal aura to appear almost more than human, as mere mortals seek to gain a little bit of this specialness, in the universal project to construct a good enough sense of self. Advertisers are wise to this, and know that conferring a transliminal glow, whether by celebrity endorsement or direct appeal to its enhancement of the self, will reliably shift the product. A moment's reflection will convince that the power of the transliminal penetrates many aspects of our lives, and if we are not aware of it, we are open to manipulation. I discuss this more fully in Clarke (2008), Chapter 12.

The logic of God

There is a fundamental feature of the transliminal that makes it quite literally impossible to pin down. It is governed by different logic. Instead of the familiar 'either/or' logic that ensures the predictability of our world, it is governed by a logic of 'both/and' – or, to use the term employed by Matte Blanco, who has explored this phenomenon, 'symmetric logic' (as a psychoanalyst he refers to the unconscious rather than the transliminal, but in this context they are equivalent). Rodney Bomford (1999), who has made Matte Blanco's (rather impenetrable) work accessible, talks about 'the logic of God'. Along with lack of time and space, this feature of the transliminal makes it radically un-navigable for us mere mortals. No wonder people like Raju get lost there.

So what might be going on here? Either/or logic is context dependent. It works perfectly within a limited compass, but if you try to stretch it, it goes fuzzy at the edges. The filter introduced by the propositional subsystem enables us to confine our gaze largely within this compass. Physics discovered this limitation when it ventured into serious exploration of the very large and distant (cosmology/general relativity) and the very small (quantum mechanics) in the 20th century. Not only does matter fail to behave according to the laws of Newtonian physics (either/or logic) at these edges; the physics required to pin down the very large and the very small is different and incompatible. Nevertheless, this physics has mathematical coherence and produces good results within its defined context. (C. Clarke 2013; Chapter 2). The slipperiness of quantum mechanics in particular never fails to fascinate (as does anything that opens a glimpse into the transliminal), and popular science writers draw conclusions from it about the elusiveness of all that is material. This is fallacious. Within the limited context, which is all we are normally concerned with, everything is as it always has been. It is only when you stray outside of that context that things get interesting.

It has already been noted that when the propositional and implicational are working together, language serves to discriminate, whereas, under more implicational influence, language also has the capacity to introduce connection. Teasdale and Barnard (1993, p. 73) contrast a poem with the same content translated into prose to make this point. We effortlessly use language in both its modes to provide colour, through associations, to our prose. However, true to the tricksterish nature of the transliminal, language can also smuggle unintended extra layers of meaning into our communication. The significance of the transliminal has long been overlooked precisely because the words used, such as psychosis and spirituality, serve to separate something that can be usefully seen as a unit.

The incompatibility of the two logics is confronted head on in paradox. We have already seen the paradoxicality of the features of the transliminal; the self is either supremely important or worthless; everything is suffused with meaning, or completely meaningless. It is no accident that religious traditions employ paradox. The paradoxical stories of Jesus (the last shall be first, etc.) and of the Zen masters alike, are designed to lead us beyond normal logic into this place.

Conclusion and summary

This exposition of the characteristics of the transliminal should be an occasion for humility. The comprehensible, either/or logic that gives us control will only take us so far. Step over the threshold, and we are in a world governed by both/and logic, that we can literally not get our minds around. Worse, there is only one world, so the one we thought we had taped is only part of the story. Scientists delude themselves when they claim that they are nearly there, merely not yet managed to cross the t's and dot the i's. There is a universe out there that science cannot master in its entirety, or even gage the extent of. When it comes to being able to grasp what is really going on, we are probably in a similar position to the degree of understanding the frogs in my pond have of my intentions for the garden.

However, once we gain more appreciation of the part that the experiential way of knowing, and in its extreme form, the transliminal, plays in our lives, we will be better able to note its operation. We will then be able to, for example, deconstruct the magnetism of the latest celebrity influencer, and so be able to mindfully resist unwanted influence; see through appeals to concepts that attract a transliminal glow and so escape manipulation. Understanding the transliminal will also make it easier to get inside the thinking of those, like Raju, who have strayed far into that unshared reality and got stuck there.

This is the point at which the next chapter will pick up the theme. Recognizing the part that this other way of knowing plays in the whole of human life paves the way for a new and less stigmatizing perspective on the phenomenon of psychosis, and fresh ways into helping people who have got lost there; appreciating that dismissing it as an illness misses the role such experiences can have in the individual's efforts to navigate through life and find their way to a more satisfactory version of themselves. Chapter 9 will outline the CCC approach to engaging with this fascinating but challenging aspect of human potential.

9 Reconfiguring mental health

Introductory summary

The previous chapter laid the groundwork for a new way of approaching the spectrum of mental health challenges, known colloquially as madness, and diagnostically as psychosis. These conditions are presented here as a normal part of the spectrum of human experiencing, for which the neutral label, 'transliminal', has been adopted. This potential for experience is often valued and sought (for instance, through spiritual practice or taking substances), but in the case of madness or psychosis, it has taken a problematic turn and become a place where someone has got stuck. This chapter will explore the way in which accessing the transliminal, or unshared reality, can be a solution that becomes a problem, in the same way that other mental health presentations have been unpacked as understandable coping strategies that can take over and intensify the distress they were intended to relieve.

Clearly, some people are more susceptible to taking the psychotic route for managing their internal state than others, and this issue will be addressed first. This susceptibility, which lies on a continuum across populations, has been labelled 'Schizotypy', and has been investigated through a substantial body of research, leading to the conclusion that high Schizotypy is associated with valued characteristics, such as creativity and spirituality, as well as conferring vulnerability to breakdown. Consideration of the conditions that create vulnerability to slipping into this unshared reality leads on naturally into ways of working clinically that use this perspective. Initiatives designed to make alternative conceptualizations of unusual and anomalous experiencing more readily available will then be introduced, along with discussion of the strand of research that demonstrates how such alternative viewpoints, sometimes accompanied by membership of a group endorsing them, leads to better outcomes for those struggling with this type of mental health issue. This adds weight to the argument that an alternative conceptualization to the medical is sorely needed in this field.

Dimension of openness to unusual experiencing

People go out of their way to follow spiritual practices, go on retreats or take substances in order to shift their consciousness towards the transliminal. For most

DOI: 10.4324/9781003081616-11

people, some specific effort is required to effect this change. However, it is much easier for some to achieve than for others, and this dimension of openness to 'anomalous experiencing', a term widely used in investigation into this field, has been extensively researched under the label of Schizotypy, by Gordon Claridge and his collaborators (see Claridge 1997 for a summary of his life's work). Claridge's Schizotypy research started from an interest in vulnerability to psychopathology, but moved into establishing openness to anomalous experiencing as a universal human dimension (Claridge 2010). Along with others, he established that high Schizotypy bestowed advantages such as high creativity and spiritual sensibility as well as the obvious vulnerability.

This finding has important clinical implications. The vulnerability can be more readily accepted and incorporated into a good enough sense of self if it can be seen to bring potential pluses as well as minuses. Understood in this way, the individual can then learn to manage that threshold between everyday and transliminal experiencing, and so take responsibility for the risk that often goes with unshared reality. Ideally, they should learn to live skilfully in both 'worlds', and draw from the strengths of each. At least, they need the skills to shut down openness to the 'other' reality and return to the consensus. Medication almost always plays a part here, but it is much better if the individual has choice and engagement in the process – is not simply 'done to'. Non-compliance with medication is widespread in this field. This is partly understandable because of the severe side effects of the neuroleptic medication used, particularly at high doses. Less recognized is ambivalence or outright reluctance to let go of the transliminal. A collaborative approach is bound to be more effective than the coercive one too often employed. Offering a more hopeful view of the situation is key to gaining this collaboration. Hopelessness destroys self-efficacy.

Research into the impact of context and conceptualization

Students of Claridge led a strand of research that took a fresh look at psychotic experience, and directly juxtaposed it with spiritual or creative expression (Chadwick, 1992, 2010; Jackson 1997, 2010), and they found strong areas of overlap. This connected with studies undertaken by Peters et al. (1999) and Peters (2010), looking at the significance of context for the impact of unusual beliefs and experiences. Chapters by all these authors are included in my edited book on psychosis and spirituality (Clarke 2010a), and their conclusions are discussed in the general interest version, 'Madness, Mystery and the Survival of God' (Clarke 2008).

More recent studies have made direct comparisons between individuals experiencing comparable anomalies or symptoms (depending on what language you are using) as measured by the standard psychiatric scales, but making sense of them in different ways. On a personal note, I was aware of this research, but it was when I heard a presentation of the conclusions reached by Caroline Brett, the researcher who really opened up the field, at a huge international conference in 2007, that I was struck forcibly by the significance of her findings for how we approach the treatment of psychosis in the health service. I resolved at that moment to use the insights I had gained exploring the overlaps with spirituality in the service of bringing change into acute care in the NHS.

This significant research (Brett et al. 2007, supervised by Peters), sets out to investigate the impact of how anomalous experiences are appraised or made sense of, the context in which they occur, and the individual's emotional response to them, on whether they lead to clinically relevant psychotic symptoms, or are managed without recourse to the mental health service.

Brett developed a scale to help explore this, and found two groups of participants, equivalent in the nature of their experiences. One set had accessed the mental health services, and the other had found various different ways to make sense of their experiences without seeking medical help. Her findings suggested that distress was reduced by developing normalizing and validating contexts in which psychotic experiences can be accepted, understood and shared. Her non-clinical participants had often found like-thinking communities who could support them through a period of breakdown in their normal life, but who made sense of what they were going through in religious, spiritual, or 'new age' ways – such as past life regression and alien abduction. It seemed that it was important not so much to eliminate the experiences, which is the goal of the conventional approach, but to be accepting of them, and be supported in making sense of them in a non-pathologizing way. Viewed from this sort of perspective, people were more motivated to take personal responsibility for managing the experiences to reduce their impact on life functioning.

This research has been extensively developed, particularly using qualitative studies, which allow for more in-depth exploration of the relationship between individuals and their unusual experiences, the sense they make of them and the impact that they have (e.g. Brett, Heriot-Maitland, McGuire & Peters, 2013, Heriot-Maitland, Knight & Peters, 2012, and Brett, Johns, Peters & McGuire, 2009). The overwhelming conclusion is that it is not so much the experiences themselves as the way they are appraised that affects how distressing, and therefore disruptive, they are. This in turn affects whether the episode can be got through with full return to normal life, or whether relapse and longer term disability results.

The importance of normalizing the experience suggested by this research fits in with the earlier work by Romme and Escher (1989) on hearing voices. A starting point for Romme and Escher was the number of people in the population who hear voices, but do not seek treatment, which they uncovered initially by means of a radio phone in. Either those people did not find hearing voices a problem (particularly if the experience was mild or sporadic), or they had found good ways of dealing with it. This prompted Romme and Escher to collect these coping strategies and disseminate them among the wider group who heard voices, including those under psychiatric care. In this way, the Hearing Voices movement of peer support groups that has taken hold all over the world was born.

Research from an epidemiological perspective backs up the suggestion that the Western psychiatric model might not be the most effective way of dealing with psychosis. Richard Warner, in his book *Recovery from Schizophrenia* (2004), which first came out in 1985, but has gone through many editions and is backed up by World Health Organization (WHO) research (Warner 2007), shows robustly how incidence of psychosis is universally the same, but that recovery rates, i.e. impact on long term life functioning, are poorer in Western than in more traditional societies. Though treatment resources in such societies are lacking, and in some cases, alarming, the overall effect of more social support and a greater tolerance and valuing of anomalous and transliminal experiences could be behind this striking discrepancy. For an in-depth anthropological exploration of these issues, see the interesting investigations by Natalie Tobert (Tobert 2017, 2014). This data points to the uncomfortable conclusion that much routine health service practice is producing iatrogenic harm.

Managing the threshold

As already covered in Chapter 2, current medical procedure, when faced with 'psychotic symptoms', is to diagnose, explain the diagnosis to the sufferer and their family, and attempt to shut down the experiences with neuroleptic medication. As the experiences can be frightening and lead to serious risk, having medication that will control them and enable the individual to access shared reality sufficiently to make two-way dialogue possible, is clearly beneficial. However, the preceding research would suggest that insisting on agreement with the diagnosis, with its accompanying gloomy prognosis and inference that any transliminal experiences, including life-enhancing ones, must be rejected and eliminated, could in fact be detrimental to health and recovery. Currently, when someone questions the illness conceptualization and their diagnosis, they are said to 'lack insight'. The research quoted above could suggest that lacking insight is no bad thing, provided responsibility for risk is shouldered, and shared reality is not totally rejected. The CCC approach in such cases therefore combines taking the need to be able to manage the threshold to unshared reality seriously, including by use of medication where necessary, along with validating alternative explanations, in a spirit of 'both/and'.

In order to be able to manage the threshold, a number of factors need to be put in place. One is motivation. It has already been suggested that having a balanced view of anomalous experiencing that does not completely demolish the sense of self, and therefore of self-efficacy, is useful here. More will be said about how to tackle this in Chapter 17. A second factor is being able to recognize which experiences are shared and which are unshared. The character of transliminal experiences, compared with everyday reality has been covered in detail in the previous chapter. The third factor is gaining an understanding of the conditions that result in someone finding themselves in unshared reality, so that these can be managed.

It has already been suggested that the transliminal way of experiencing can be deliberately produced by taking substances or by particular practices. Psychedelic substances such as LSD are primarily associated with this sort of 'trip', and cannabis has this effect on those who are more susceptible. Looking at spiritual practices, across the board, certain themes emerge. Music, rhythm, repetition (ritual), chanting and vocalizing, and sometimes dance are involved in many, usually but not exclusively, communal practices. There is clearly something about giving oneself up to rhythmic activity that shifts people across the threshold. Raves, trance dances and the like use this. Substances, communally ingested, are also often involved, whether in ayahuasca ceremonies, ecstasy and raves, or in a tokenistic form, communion wine in Christian churches.

The other sort of spiritual practice associated with entry into the transliminal is solitary and involves sensory deprivation. Extensive meditation practice, isolation, silence, severe limitation of food (fasting), sleep disruption – the monastic practice of getting up for services in the middle of the night: all these are familiar to monastic and retreat regimes, designed to shut down the everyday mental chatter and either transport the devotee into a place of relationship with that which is beyond (how that is understood will depend on the context) or deeper into their own being. Interestingly, all these routes into the transliminal are mirrored in the sort of conditions that tend to precede a psychotic breakdown. Isolation; sleep deprivation; not eating properly or at all, are regularly noted in those arriving in acute mental health services with psychotic symptoms. Those finding their way to these services have not had the benefit of the holding routine of a monastic community to contain them through their crisis.

The role of life events

A common factor in catapulting people over the threshold into the transliminal is the impact of events. The role of life events in precipitating mental breakdown is obvious and has long been recognized (Bebbington et al. 1993). High Schizotypy, which entails easy access to the transliminal, is associated with acute sensitivity. For sensitive people, life transitions that would be seen as normal or positive for many, such as leaving home in late adolescence for work or study for instance, can precipitate breakdown. Childbirth is a time of opening and heightened emotion for most. It has the potential to take some women dangerously into unshared reality. There is a growing body of compelling evidence about the connection between asylum seeking, migration, displacement, racism and social adversity and psychotic breakdown, leading to over-representation of the ethnically diverse in services (Rosenfield, 2012, Kirkbride et al. 2012, Heinz, Deserno & Reininghaus, 2013).

Discussion of the impact of trauma across time (Chapter 5) demonstrates how distant events can intensify the effect of current life events. Evidence for the incidence of trauma in those presenting to services with psychotic symptoms is mounting (Varese et al. 2012, Read & Bentall 2012, Longden, Madill & Waterman 2012), and eroding the credibility of the line of argument that schizophrenia is an illness, with genetic predisposition, like diabetes, and nothing more. Nor is this factor confined to those who acquire a diagnosis. The Christian spiritual literature, the lives of the saints, confirms that life events have a role to play in precipitating mystical experience; Julian of Norwich and

Hildegard of Bingen both received their first visions, later in life, when recovering from serious illness.

Potential for growth

There is also evidence from the many people who have powerful transliminal experiences, including those where their lives are not sufficiently disrupted to be identified as a problem, that earlier trauma somehow facilitates crossing the threshold. As noted in the previous chapter, the way boundaries within the self are broken down by the experience can precipitate re-emergence of problematic experiences that had been buried or side-lined. While this can lead to a mental breakdown, it also offers an opportunity to deal with issues that are a barrier to personal growth and realization of potential. Another important theme follows from this; the role of crossing over or escaping into the transliminal as a response to a stuck situation; a response which has the potential to offer a way forward, but can equally plunge the individual into recurring psychosis and dependence on services.

Mike Jackson (1997, 2010) one of the first psychologists to research the overlap between spiritual and psychotic experiences, talks of accessing the transliminal as 'problem solving'. Someone has encountered circumstances in their life that overwhelm their capacity to cope, and the transliminal offers a 'way out', or an escape from an intolerable situation – in the same way that withdrawal (depression) and rumination (anxiety disorders) are responses to unmanageable emotion.

Sometimes, the transliminal experience offers a way forward that leads to a fuller and better life. There are many instances of this in the spiritual literature. Both Buddha and St Francis of Assisi, for instance, were dissatisfied with the hedonistic life style of a young prince or nobleman and were jolted out of this by revelation. Interestingly, St Francis started off his new direction on the wrong tack, taking God's instruction to 'rebuild my church', literally, by launching into construction work on a ruined chapel – until God put him right and set him on the much more ambitious task of reviving the whole of Christian ministry in the 13 century, through the radical poverty and compassion practiced by the Franciscan order he founded.

This positive potential for transliminal experiences was picked up by the influential spiritual emergence/emergency movement, started by Stanislav Grof (e.g. Grof & Grof 1991). The Grofs favoured inducing such experiences in order to further growth and personal transformation, first by use of LSD, and later, holotropic breathing. Ideally this process enabled a gentle and manageable 'emergence'. However, the Grofs also recognized spontaneously occurring transliminal experiences as paralleling this process, and that both these and the induced experiences could get out of hand, thus becoming 'emergency'. The Grofs claimed there was a distinction between such spiritual emergencies and psychosis. It is this distinction that is being challenged here, and the UK Spiritual Crisis Network, which offers online support and an alternative conceptualization to the illness model for people going through such experiences, explicitly rejects this distinction (www.spiritua

lcrisisnetwork.uk). As well as my work within the NHS, I am a volunteer director of SCN, in order to ensure that this lifeline is available.

Jackson (2010) tracks how this process of accessing the transliminal when the ordinary course of life becomes blocked, can easily go astray, resulting in someone becoming stuck on the wrong side of the threshold. Unshared experiences can cut people off from those around them. The new experience of vulnerability and openness can lead them to shut themselves away, safe from stimulation and invasion. Looking after themselves can cease to be a priority, leading to all the sensory and physical deprivation conditions designed to drive a human being further into the unshared world. At the same time, they are no longer on the same wavelength as others, who see their fervent preoccupations as mad. Their sense of self will already have become fluid, as seen in the previous chapter, but the devalued status offered to someone with a psychiatric diagnosis is sufficiently unappealing to make even a quite frightening and unpleasant unshared reality appear more attractive.

Powerful medication, given to shut down the experiences, can take away someone's ability to pick up their normal life, through dulling cognition and sapping energy. The resulting retreat from the shared world is not worked out by propositional logic, but more driven by desperation. This is how opening to the transliminal, with its potential for growth and development, can lead to someone becoming stuck in the psychiatric system. This danger points to the urgent need for ways of helping people struggling with these experiences that does not drive them deeper into dysfunction. How this can be achieved will be looked from the CCC perspective in Chapter 17.

Now let us turn to the real danger facing Raju and Ambika. Ambika is frightened and at her wits' end. Raju doesn't see the need to involve the doctor. Once in the service he is pretty sure to be given a diagnosis of schizophrenia or similar. What will that do to his already fragile sense of self?

Raju

As Raju refused to see the GP, Ambika asked the doctor for help, only to learn that nothing could be done without Raju's consent, unless risk had reached a sufficient threshold to warrant the involvement of a Mental Health Act team. This team would consist of an approved Mental Health Act assessor (usually a social worker) and a doctor, who would have the power to admit someone to hospital and administer treatment (medication) against their will. Ambika did not want to make a big deal out of the moment when she had been frightened of Raju's anger; all was quiet if contentious subjects were avoided. All she wanted was for a professional to talk to him and suggest how he might be helped.

Things drifted on for months. Raju was withdrawn and preoccupied most of the time, but sometimes elated and excited, living in his own world. Ambika let him talk about it when he wanted to, but did not probe or react much. Some of what he talked about pertained to Hindu mythology – the background faith of the couple, which had only played a part in their lives on family occasions up until now. Ambika did persuade him to meet the most scholarly of the Hindu priests at their local temple for a discussion. The talk did not go well, as the priest did not fall in with Raju's perspective, and reported to Ambika that the ideas were grandiose and outside of his orthodox practice.

Ambika became more worried when Raju started to talk about his mission being under attack, and hearing voices ordering him to kill himself. She was therefore really alarmed when she returned late from work one day to find he had vanished. Desperate, she phoned everyone she could think of: the police, the GP, all his family, and then set off to try and find him. Calculation or instinct led her to a local railway bridge, where she found him, preparing himself to jump when the next train approached. He agreed to return home with her, where they found assembled his father, mother and a couple of brothers – who took control of the situation and involved the mental health team, with Ambika's reluctant agreement. This led to an emergency assessment, Raju's forcible removal and admission to hospital under a section of the Mental Health Act. This meant he could be detained and given sedating medication against his will. Ambika was at the same time relieved and worried about what would happen next.

Conclusion and summary

The book is primarily about mental health breakdown, and entering a psychotic state is one of the most serious forms that breakdown can take. The person you are concerned about might well become different, unreachable and in more serious cases, risk rears its head. This can be understandably disturbing and frightening, and when we are afraid, we crave certainty and simplicity. A diagnosis, and medication with compliance enforced legally provides just that. In cases of immediate risk, there is no alternative, as we have seen with the example of Raju.

This chapter has argued that this simple solution, though it might be unavoidable in the short term, does not do justice to the full picture of what is happening here, and needs to be balanced with other perspectives if the individual is to get through the episode to good recovery, as opposed to a half-life of relapse and control by the mental health services.

It would be unfair to say that the mental health service response to someone displaying symptoms of psychosis is always as coercive as the example given here, though where immediate risk is involved, it is likely to be. The hospital experience will improve for Raju, as will be seen in Chapter 17. Early Intervention in Psychosis services are available throughout the UK, and they endeavour to link psychological with medical treatment, and to take into full account the needs of the individual. There is an exciting recent development imported from Finland, called Open Dialogue (Seikkula et al. 2006), that allows everyone, the service user, the family and anyone else involved, to have a voice, and takes seriously the way the individual at the heart of it makes sense of their situation. This is currently available in a few NHS sites in the UK and is undergoing a major trial, so should hopefully be rolled out more widely in the future (Razzaque & Wood 2015). It would meet many of my criticisms of the service if it is.

For the present, there is a need for wider awareness of the points made in the chapter, for the sake of a good outcome for people who experience this type of breakdown.

- The Schizotypy spectrum representing a universal potential to access the transliminal, that links the need to manage vulnerability with gifts that can go with that vulnerability.
- The recognition that breakdown can be the route to breakthrough; the spiritual emergence/emergency and Spiritual Crisis Network perspectives.
- The importance of ways of making sense of the experiences that do not shatter the self, ideally supported by a community of other people, even if those ideas are not scientifically respectable.

All these factors are important to bear in mind, even when the crisis is at its height and can only be managed by heavy, medical intervention. There is a bigger and much more hopeful vista beyond, that the individual can be helped to discover and benefit from.

This chapter concludes this section of the book, which has explored CCC in depth. In the next section, we home in on how CCC can help an individual make sense of their predicament in ways that are understanding and sympathetic about their coping so far, while at the same time offering more positive coping strategies in order to escape from a stuck situation and take life forwards.

Section III

How to help: Comprehend and Cope

The next two sections take the reader through the process of a CCC therapy. This is quite structured, at the same time as being built on whatever the individual brings. The next seven chapters introduce the approach, and then illustrate it by applying it to our three composite case examples. These sections are not designed as a manual for the therapy. Such a manual is included in Clarke & Nicholls (2018). Rather, it outlines the process and gives a feel for what it is like and what it can achieve. Some readers may be interested in the approach as therapists, but the book has a wider aim; to shape conceptualization about what is going on in the case of mental health breakdown; to enable the supporter to empathize accurately with the individual in breakdown, and to identify what is most likely to be helpful. Therapy is always only the tip of an iceberg. The mass is composed of all those roles, relationships and connections in the person's natural life. The more sympathetic understanding and helpful support can be offered by those constituting the mass of the iceberg, the better for the sufferer.

DOI: 10.4324/9781003081616-12

Section III

How to help: Comprehend and Cope

10 Meeting someone from the inside and getting the mind in gear

Introductory summary

Many therapy approaches start with an individual formulation, which summarizes the cause and effect of whatever the client is experiencing. For instance, a CBT formulation will identify the way that the problem is maintained, and, where a longitudinal formulation is adopted, add relevant factors from the history. In CCC, the formulation 'Comprehend' lies at the heart of the therapy. However, this is not something to plunge into without due preparation. This chapter covers the preparatory phase, which comprises three important elements. First and foremost, the individual needs to tell their story and be heard. This is not a formulation arrived at by asking a set of questions and filling in boxes. It needs to reflect what is most vital and emotionally live for that individual. It omits a lot of the extraneous detail gathered in the conventional psychological therapy assessment interview. It homes in on what makes that person tick, and the individual must feel heard and understood. This is the essential foundation for the challenging journey that therapist and client have ahead of them.

Secondly, the therapist needs to explain the States of Mind diagram (Figure 1.1) and the way in which the past can intrude upon the present. For most people, this enables them to understand why current circumstances have hit them hard, and to be more forgiving of themselves, as well as conveying the essence of the theoretical basis for the approach. In the case of anomalous experiencing (psychosis), the diagram will include shared and unshared reality (Figure 8.1).

The third task follows naturally from this. It is introducing the skill of grounding mindfulness in order to navigate the emotional and reasonable minds in the diagram, and the skill of bringing level of arousal down through breathing, which will bring the two together.

Preparing to formulate – the wider application of the formulation

The CCC approach hinges on a simple formulation, grounded firmly in felt sense and emotion, and factoring in life events, situation and past trauma, naming strengths and values, before homing in on the vicious cycles that need

DOI: 10.4324/9781003081616-13

to be breached if the individual is to break free of mental anguish, and in most cases, break free of the past. The formulation was developed to be worked out collaboratively with someone experiencing mental health crisis, in a one-to-one session. It has since proved to have usefulness in far wider contexts. Within mental health services, from acute inpatient to primary care and everything in-between, it is used to give teams a compassionate understanding of the people under their care; an understanding that provides practical guidance on the ways forward (Clarke 2015). It has wider applicability for enabling those supporting people undergoing mental health breakdown to make sense of it from the perspective of the person suffering. This does not imply embarking on therapy, but can both provide insight into the type of support that the individual might need, and gives clues as to useful approaches; what to say in an interaction. With this in mind, the chapters in this section will give a thorough idea of how a CCC therapy is approached, but not as a straight manual. There is such a manual for the therapy in the central section of Clarke & Nicholls (2018).

When working with an individual, the way in which a relationship is built up before the formulation can be approached is crucial. The formulation is straight-forward, so someone with experience of working in this way will start to identify the vicious cycles that the person is tangled up in, the circumstances producing the intolerable feeling, etc. quite quickly after meeting them. This is not the time to share that insight. There is ground work to be done first. The quality of the rela-tionship is the foundation on which everything must be built. Later on, it could be necessary to be quite challenging. This can only be done if trust has been built, and the whole enterprise feels truly owned by both parties. Open-minded, compas-sionate listening is the way in; following what that person feels is important and is prepared to talk about, validating their feelings and actions, and giving permission to either disclose, or hint at and leave sensitive areas unspoken.

This feels very different from the sort of assessment that probes for a lot of information, and it requires a preparedness to leave areas unexplored; fascinat-ing questions unasked. This avoids potential pitfalls – the standard history taking procedure can be seriously un-therapeutic. Painful details do not need to be probed for the story to have been heard. Sensitivity and attention to the individual are the watchwords here. The exception is anything pertaining to risk, which must be probed and established as a duty of care. The main focus of the listener is to get inside the experience, to be able to validate honestly the choices made, even where these are less than optimal, to reflect the feelings, and to look out for and name courage, achievement and survival.

The CCC therapist, while encouraging their client to talk about anything relevant to their having presented in crisis or otherwise in need of help, will of course be looking out for the elements that will go into the formulation: their emotions; the immediate circumstances that have led to breakdown; informa-tion about the past that will have contributed to the unbearable feeling; their strengths, values and potential, and the ways in which they are currently coping. All these will need to be explored more precisely when the time to construct the diagram arrives. Our three case examples can illustrate this stage.

Kath

Kath has been referred to the local IAPT service. IAPT services are available across England and provide predominantly, but not exclusively, CBT. CCC (which is a branch of CBT), where available, is indicated when other approaches have been tried previously, without lasting benefit, and where the past appears to be a complicating factor. In her first session, Kath pours out the story of her situation. There are realistic fears of violence from the man she was recently involved with, who is harassing and essentially stalking her. She is in a dilemma over her mother whose dementia is getting progressively worse and she worries that her father is physically and mentally abusing her mother as his short temper ill equips him for the role of carer. She would love to take more of a role in her mother's care, but she needs to keep her job to survive financially, and she has her daughter to care for. Also, she does not dare say anything that might be construed as criticism by her irascible father. Her father rules out the care home option on grounds of expense. To cap it all, there is change at work, with a new manager, Cheryl, brought in to shake things up, who has little appreciation of Kath's strengths and sees her as a problem. Kath, who is aware of her effectiveness at the job, and was invited to go for the managerial role, but lacked the confidence, feels Cheryl is being unfair and targeting her.

The therapist notes Kath's father's difficult temperament and wonders what it was like growing up in that household. This leads to the story of her miserable childhood at home, compounded by being bullied at school, as a socially awkward and withdrawn only child. Escape into an abusive marriage followed. The therapist comments on Kath's strength and courage in breaking free from that marriage, and being a devoted mother and effective employee, contrasting with the example of her own mother whose life was dominated by an abusive husband.

The therapist then returned to the stalker, and finding that Kath had not alerted the police, encouraged her to collect texts and record sightings in preparation for requesting the protection that the situation clearly merited.

Tasha

With her diagnosis of Borderline Personality Disorder, Tasha was referred to the DBT service, who provide an intensive year long programme, but they failed to engage and secure the required commitment from her. When she presented again to the Community Mental Health service with more concerning self-harm, she was referred to the team's clinical psychologist, to see if CCC might work.

Getting Tasha to attend an appointment was not easy. She cancelled two at the last minute with rather feeble excuses. On the phone with the therapist, she pleaded fear of going to new places on her own, but was prepared to attend with a friend. At her first session, friend in tow, she came across as defiant rather than anxious, and appeared ready to dismiss the therapy out of hand. However, when she got onto the subject of her profoundly learning disabled brother, Tasha really opened up, and the therapist encouraged her to talk at length about how she understood him and could manage him, much better than her mother, and how much she cared for him. Feeling the therapist's real interest in what concerned her, and her validation of her skill and caring, she was prepared to come back again, on her own. At the second session, she opened up more about her self-harm, which she had learnt in childhood as a way to manage the anger and disgust she felt at the abuse. Her strongest anger, however, seemed reserved for her mother who had failed to protect her, and was so taken up with her disabled son that Tasha was left out, and not given credit for her real contribution to the challenge of managing her brother.

At the same time she was protective towards her mother, who had multiple health needs. The therapist commented that Tasha seemed wholly taken up with caring for others and wondered what she felt about looking after herself and about her future. Tasha vehemently declared that she had no time for herself; she was a waste of space, she hated herself.

The strongest feelings came out when the psychologist asked about what might have led to the recent escalation of self-harm. Tasha's tough shell cracked as she explained it was the anniversary of her nan's death. Through tears she explained that Nan had taken care of her for her first eight years – until her mother had got together with the abuser, who had persuaded her mother to 'complete the family' by bringing her daughter back to live with them. That had been a brutal wrench. Tasha had tried to keep in touch with her nan over the years; difficult because she lived at a distance. Her nan's death the year before was unbearable to think about, and self-harm enabled her to switch to coping with the easier, physical, pain. This painful sharing cemented the therapeutic alliance, and Tasha was committed to continuing to attend sessions.

Raju

Raju, having been found by Ambika on the bridge, preparing to jump in front of a train, had been admitted to hospital under an emergency section. He was very angry and not very communicative, but Ambika explained to the team what had been going on, and he was forcibly given sedative medication. After some days pacing around the ward, declaring that he had an important mission and they had no right to detain him as he was not mentally ill, he was referred to the ward's clinical psychologist. She encouraged him to talk about his preoccupations. He told her about the internet sites he had been visiting, until he found he could communicate directly with higher spheres without the need for a computer. After listening for a while, she asked about Ambika and his ordinary life. He said that he had contempt for the accountancy jobs he had been doing that were beneath him. About Ambika, he said that at first he was just sad that she didn't understand. Now he was angry that she had betrayed him to 'the enemy' by sanctioning his sectioning.

The psychologist commented how frustrating it must be for him that all this was so important for him, but no one else saw it that way. She wondered whether he experienced it as if he were somehow on a different wavelength from the others. That did strike a chord, and gave her a way in to gently introduce the ideas of shared and unshared reality.

Introducing the model

As well as establishing a trusting relationship and gaining an in-depth knowledge of the experience and concerns of the individual, the therapist needs to put a couple of elements in place before embarking on the formulation. Validating the person's current coping through linking it to the 'States of Mind' diagram (Figure 1.1), which is the bedrock of the approach is one.

This is how the therapist introduced it to Kath.

TH: It is very understandable, given what has been going on, that you have been unable to shake off the depression, and that Cheryl's arrival at work has been so difficult for you. As human beings we constantly manage a balancing act between the part of our mind that deals with emotion, relationship and joins things up, and the other part that works things out exactly and separates them [points out Emotion and Reasonable Mind]. Important roles and relationships help us to keep that balance and to feel alright. When things change, it can be hard or impossible to keep that balance. Some people are naturally more sensitive than others, so keeping the balance is always hard for them. This is a simplified diagram of how the brain is wired up. Most of the time the two circles work together, and we can find 'Wise Mind'. However, when things are really difficult, they tend to separate and you get left with the emotional part in charge. As you see from the diagram, they have different memories, and the emotional part stores memories for threat separate from the Reasonable part of the mind that manages things like time and place. This means that when something bad happens now, it sparks off the bad memory from the past, and it can even be experienced as if it were happening now. This makes present difficulties harder to bear and the feelings tend to take over. In your case, fear of the man pursuing you takes you back both to your father and to your ex. You have already said that Cheryl feels like the bullies at school whom you could never escape.

K: I had never thought of it like that. I do find myself feeling like I did at school at work these days, and when I hear my father shouting at my poor mother, that helplessness about being able to do nothing is like it was for me when I was little.

Tasha was similarly able to begin to see why she felt so devastated by the anniversary of her nan's death, when she realized that it took her back to the terrible time when she was eight years old, taken out of a home where, though not perfect – Nan had her problems – she was loved and cared for, to one where her mother did not really want her and her stepfather abused and terrified her. Before, she had berated herself as stupid. She couldn't understand why she had been able to manage quite well at the time, through the funeral, etc. but then collapsed over it a year later. Now she could begin to see how this made sense.

Raju's case was a bit different. His section of the Mental Health Act meant that he could be held and medicated against his will for 28 days initially, but with the possibility of that being extended to six months if risk persisted. However, the psychiatrist wanted to get his cooperation before administering an injection (called a depot) with a long lasting dose of neuroleptic medication, designed to bring him back to shared reality (usually accompanied by a more general shutting down and other side effects). Along with the rest of the multi-disciplinary team, the psychologist had a key role here. She did not attempt to set up formal therapy sessions, but rather caught up with him for short chats whenever she was on the ward. Often these were about what he was doing; the occupational therapist had managed to get him doing art work – something he had loved as a boy, but abandoned as it did not fit with the family's expectations. She also listened to his preoccupations and dropped in things about shared and unshared reality. One day she reached the breakthrough conversation as follows:

R: So you don't believe me when you say all this is 'unshared'.
CP: Look, I really don't know. None of us knows much about reality for certain, we are limited as human beings. You are right that I tend to go with the consensus, but that doesn't I rule out your reality. I know it is real for you, and I think it could be saying important things, but not straightforwardly. Unshared reality is governed by a different logic – one of both/and, where contradictory things can be valid at the same time. So what it is telling you might be a bit wrapped up in riddles. For instance, it seems to be saying that you need to be doing something different from accountancy; that life might work better for you and you could be more successful if you did. What do you think?
R: I certainly can't go back to a reality where I have to be an accountant!
CP: But you cannot abandon shared reality altogether. You need both. Look at this diagram [Figure 8.1].
This is how everybody's mind is wired up. These two circles separate for a while when we are asleep and dream; they separate a bit at other times, when you are wrapped up in something – like your drawing, for instance. When they totally separate, you find yourself in a different reality. You have travelled further than most into that other possible reality. We all need to take both realities seriously. For instance, Ambika loves you and does not want to lose you over there. She is worried. Because the mental health team are worried, you have been detained in hospital, and so are not in control of your life. You need to learn to pass between the two realities, back and forth. If you can do that, you do not need to lose the other one completely, just keep it in its place. Will you think about that?
R: OK. That is quite interesting. I will take the diagram away and think about it.

The last element to be put in place before embarking on the formulation is to introduce breathing and grounding mindfulness as immediate ways to be able to achieve an observer position in relation to both emotion and reasonable minds; in other words, to regain wise mind. More will be said about that in Chapter 12.

Conclusion and summary

This chapter has laid the essential groundwork for the CCC approach to therapy. Our three case examples have had an opportunity to tell their stories, following what was most salient for them. This has given the therapist the information needed to embark on a collaborative formulation in the cases of Kath and Tasha. In Raju's case, it has meant suggesting an alternative way of looking at what he was experiencing that might offer the opportunity to build a therapeutic alliance. As we shall see, however, things were still at a very fragile stage in his case, and dependent on the wider system. Kath and Tasha have also been introduced to the emotion mind/reasonable mind model and to the practice of mindfulness, to gain the observer perspective which is a pre-condition to addressing stuck patterns of responding. Above all, all three were engaged, so that progressing to the next stage becomes possible.

The next chapter will introduce the formulation at the heart of CCC, illustrated by Kath and Tasha's diagrams and the process behind their construction. Such a diagram would not be indicated in the case of Raju. He was too distant from shared reality for that, even had it been possible to maintain the therapeutic alliance in the face of developments in the wider system.

11 Comprehend

Introducing the spiky diagram

Introductory summary

This chapter covers the construction of the formulation diagram, placing the feeling, the internal state, at its heart. Even if this is not fully articulated it can be inferred from the way in which the individual is dealing with their unbearable emotions (e.g. self-harm is their usual way of managing intolerable feelings). The recent events that might have caused this internal state then need to be explored, and, with sensitivity, past threat situations that will have been re-activated by present troubles.

Having outlined the problem areas, it is now necessary to summarize a full picture of the individual in all their strengths, passions and potential, along with containing relationships, including faith or spiritual connection where relevant. This is entered onto the 'strengths bow' of the diagram.

The diagram is completed with the identification of the vicious cycles; precise behavioural analysis of how the individual is currently coping that includes how this helps in the short term, but enables the individual themselves to recognize the way in which that coping ultimately feeds the intolerable feeling and keeps them stuck. These cycles provide the vital clues as to how change is to be achieved. Current coping needs validating at the same time as encouraging recognition of how it keeps them trapped.

Launching into the diagram

Once the individual has been encouraged to share what is important for them and to tell their story, the spiky diagram formulation can be embarked upon. The manual in Clarke & Nicholls 2018 for an IAPT CCC programme, stipulates that this should be done in session two, and it is a good idea not to dither too long. The manual follows the course of a CCC therapy in our IAPT service, where the formulation is normally completed in four individual sessions, to be followed by a 12-week group programme. Having said that, writing this in the midst of the COVID-19 pandemic, when therapy must be conducted over the internet, I am letting my clients have the odd extra session before launching them into the, now virtual, group experience.

In Acute services, a second session can be a luxury, so rapid is throughput in psychiatric inpatient units nowadays. Bullock et al. (2020) is an example of an evaluation study of formulation completed at the end of session one. On the other hand, it

DOI: 10.4324/9781003081616-14

might be necessary to spend longer than a session on the engagement process. Tasha is an example of this, and in Raju's case, the therapy is conducted without a diagram, but informed by the logic of the formulation. The process will now be illustrated by taking the reader through the construction of Kath and Tasha's diagrams.

Kath's diagram

The process of working out this diagram started with the therapist commenting on the overwhelming feelings that Kath must be experiencing in the light of all that was going on, and then drawing an uneven, jagged shape on a piece of paper (much less neat than the printed version; however, now that therapy is conducted online because of COVID-19, we are using this template). The therapist declared his intention to represent these emotions with the most horrible shape he knew how to draw. The circumstances producing those emotions, both recent and past, were worked out together, and entered into boxes with arrows leading to the feelings. Getting Kath to focus on her strengths was a bit challenging; these were written curving around the bow. When asked, Kath said that she did not practise a faith, but felt that she was a spiritual person and this was important to her. She identified feeling a sense of deeper connection when she was in nature, and could see that shutting herself away cut her off from this. Once the strengths and connections were in place, the strategies she used to cope at present were worked out carefully, with due attention to the reasons why they made sense. Questioning what happened next gently led Kath into explaining how the strategy then took her back into the spiky feeling and reinforced it.

The vicious circles are important as they are the part of the diagram that will determine the course of the therapy. The boxes around the recent and distant past represent the fact that these are circumstances that need to be accepted before the individual can move on. There are no borders around the stages of the maintaining cycle, because this is the part that can be changed. The principles of behaviourism underpin identifying the cycles, an important scientific building block of psychological theory. Emotion is given a central role in CCC, but so is behaviour. Experimental science established in detail how behaviour is maintained and shaped by its consequences and antecedents. These consequences and antecedents need clear identification as a first step to altering the behaviour. Behavioural therapies proceed by constructing a careful behavioural analysis. In DBT this is called a chain analysis and in CCC it is the vicious circle part of the formulation diagram.

The emotion, driven by the earlier circumstances, is the first step in the behavioural analysis, leading to the coping strategy used to manage it. This is reinforced by something, or it would not have become a repeated pattern. We do things that make sense or help. In Kath's case, it is easier to withdraw when she feels low, and self-criticism feels right; it is what she has learnt. Naming this is normalizing and helps the person to feel understood, and therefore more ready to track the way in which the strategy rebounds, actually making worse the feeling it was designed to mitigate, thus keeping the individual trapped. It is really important that this learning comes as much as possible from the client him or herself and is therefore owned by them, not imposed.

Asked for her reaction, Kath could see that the diagram made sense. She felt less useless as it had been recognized that she was really trying, but that there was a lot dragging her down. She could understand the need to break the cycles and was ready to start thinking about that.

Kath´s Formulation Diagram

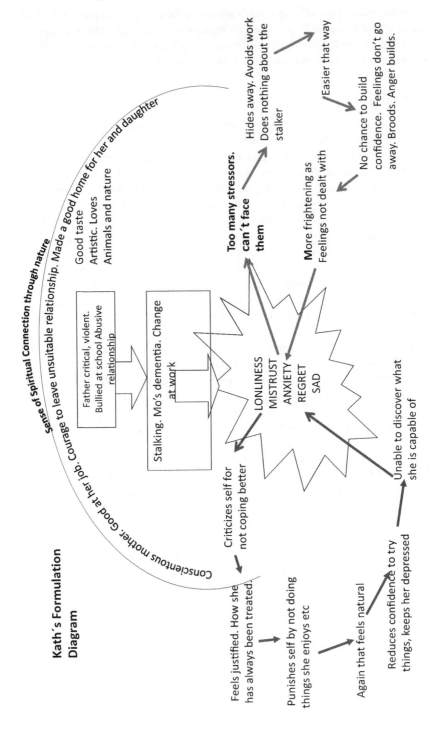

Sense of Spiritual Connection through nature. Made a good home for her and daughter

Good taste Artistic. Loves Animals and nature

Father critical, violent. Bullied at school Abusive relationship

Stalking. Mo's dementia. Change at work

LONLINESS
MISTRUST
ANXIETY
REGRET
SAD

Too many stressors. can´t face them

Hides away. Avoids work Does nothing about the stalker

Easier that way

More frightening as Feelings not dealt with

No chance to build confidence. Feelings don't go away. Broods. Anger builds.

Criticizes self for not coping better

Conscientous mother. Good at her job. Courage to leave unsuitable relationship.

Unable to discover what she is capable of

Feels justified. How she has always been treated

Punishes self by not doing things she enjoys etc

Again that feels natural

Reduces confidence to try things, keeps her depressed

Figure 11.1 Kath's Diagram

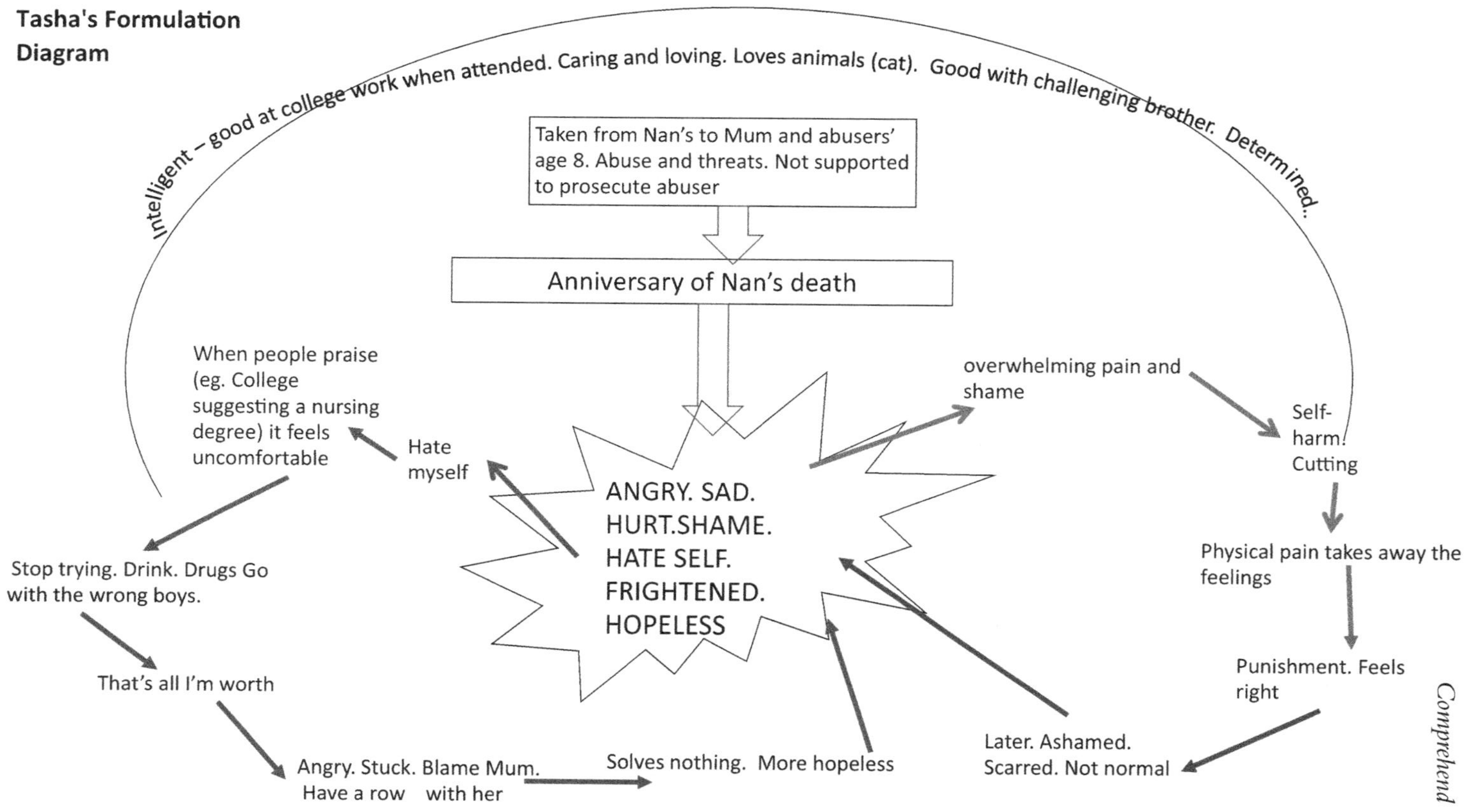

Tasha's Formulation Diagram

Figure 11.2 Tasha's Diagram

Tasha's diagram

Getting an agreed diagram for Tasha was more of a struggle. She would launch into the task with enthusiasm, coming up with so many feelings that it was hard to fit them all in, and then draw back; suddenly reluctant to acknowledge that she had any choices, declaring that self-harm was the only thing that stopped her killing herself, and suddenly becoming protective of her mother when she felt she was being criticized by the therapist. When it came to identifying the strengths, Tasha readily agreed about her caring nature, but admitting her academic and career potential was more difficult. She had already told the therapist about the college's encouragement to set her sights higher, but initially when the therapist recalled this and wanted to put it down, she drew back, saying that it was all rubbish. However, in the end, over two sessions, they did manage to agree on a diagram that Tasha admitted summed it all up pretty well.

Raju

At this stage, things were going backwards for Raju. A weekend and a couple of days had elapsed since his last meeting with the psychologist, who only worked half the week on the ward. When she approached Raju again, he angrily refused to speak with her, saying she didn't believe him and was just like the rest. The nurse in the office gave the back story. Raju's section had been extended to one lasting six months, and he had been warned that if he did not accept medication voluntarily, he would be forcibly medicated next day. His previous psychiatrist had gone on leave, and the colleague who took over did not agree with the cautious approach, arguing that evidence showed duration of untreated psychosis should be as short as possible. Raju's reaction now made sense.

Breaking the cycles

For Kath, the diagram demonstrated immediately that she needed to resist the urge to hide away and brood when she felt low, and to start being less self-critical; to become generally nicer to herself, and allow herself to do things she enjoyed as well as things she ought to do. She was willing to try, but at this stage she could not see how she could manage any of that.

Tasha was much more ambivalent. She could see the logic alright, but was convinced that self-harm was the only safe way to manage her feelings and keep suicidal urges at bay. She dismissed the idea of treating herself better, because that would not accord with how she felt; it would be false, and anyway she didn't deserve it.

The next phase of the therapy, after ways of breaking the circles and the goals for therapy have been agreed is to introduce skills to make this possible. However, as already indicated in the case of mindfulness and breathing, some skills need to be taught earlier on, and it was important to get across to Kath that it was understandable that being asked to approach things completely differently was daunting, and that she would be given plenty of help and support for it. A possible way forward was set out for her to consider as follows. This would inform the goals that were later agreed once she was happy with it.

1   A balanced approach to challenging the depression.

- On the one side she did need to give herself a push to do things she might be avoiding.
- On the other, she needed to be kind and understanding with herself, acknowledging that this was really difficult while she was feeling low; she needed to give herself full credit for managing anything and not compare herself when depressed with herself at her best. She needed to allow herself down time without giving herself a hard time about it.
- Once she had got herself into this wise mind place, she had a better chance of meeting head on and problem solving the accumulation of immediate stresses and real-world issues that she faced.

2   To challenge the self-criticism, she needed to treat herself as she would treat a good friend – more will be said about that later. The two are of course linked.

Once this had been explained, Kath was prepared to sign up to pursuing these two points as goals of the therapy. The therapist was aware that he had not addressed Kath's anger, and was holding that in reserve as something to be tackled later, not least because of its potential as a useful resource, but probably not something that Kath was ready to recognize just yet.

In Tasha's case, the therapist approached the task of negotiating goals, referring to the diagram which was on a table between them, as follows:

TH: This idea that you are a waste of space, I wonder if you got that because of how you were treated here [points to the past box]?

TA: Mm.

TH: You are pretty angry at both your stepdad for what he did, and your mum, because she wouldn't support you to confront him, weren't you, and as I see it, in the circumstances, that anger is absolutely justified. However, it sounds as though you have taken over not valuing yourself from the way they treated you. Do you really want them to win like that? That wouldn't be what your nan would have wanted. When you carry on going round the circle here, you are keeping the bad past alive in your life. Isn't there a part of you that would like to be rid of it?

TA: Mm. But it has always been like that. Thinking of Nan just hurts, so I try not to.

TH: I can appreciate that. When you are feeling brave, we need to set aside some time to talk about Nan. I think she is really important here. Though she is no longer with us, how she treated you, how she felt about you, remains an important part of you – and it could be the part you need to go forward. Does that make sense?

TA: Sort of, but scary.

TH: That is so understandable, but have you noticed how, when you get into the habit of avoiding something, it gets more scary, and you feel less confident to face it the longer that goes on for? However, we can take things at the pace that feels manageable for you. At least now we have a clue about how to move forward. It could be that if you follow how your nan treated you instead of carrying on treating yourself badly like the others, things could be different, and to make things different is why you are coming here, isn't it?

TA: Yes.

TH: So, following on from that, attacking yourself by self-harming really would not make sense if you are trying to free yourself from the abuser. Then, following what your tutors say you are capable of, and going for an access course and a nursing degree would make sense – that would show them, wouldn't it? That would mean you could really help your brother and kids like him. Your mum would have to take notice then.

TA: OK. That would be good. But it sounds hard.

TH: College thinks you could do it. First things first. Let's have another go at that grounding mindfulness we tried last week, as you need a way to stop yourself and choose to do something different when you feel the urge to self-harm. Are you prepared to have a go at that?

TA: Alright. [Mindfulness follows.]

TH: Between now and next time, think if you would be ready to say a bit more about Nan, and to have a good cry, because what happened is truly sad. It needs those tears, and we are given tears to help us come to terms with things that can feel unbearable.

Negotiating goals

Once the cycles have been established and ways of breaking them agreed, clear behavioural goals can be negotiated, and laid down. This is an important stage, as those goals will shape the course of the rest of the therapy which will be about learning and trying out skills. There is a noticeable change of gear in the therapy at this point. The formulation stage is about being open to where that individual is coming from and working out with them collaboratively the content of the diagram. While ambivalence is normal, there needs to be overall agreement about the rationale and the way forward, which is translated into the specific goals. This does not rule out adding to the diagram or the cycles and goals as new information emerges, or the individual becomes ready to meet further challenge. As indicated in Kath's case, an anger cycle would almost certainly be needed, but that had to emerge when she was ready for it. Tasha required quite a bit of motivation work before she was prepared to commit to goals, and was bound to present with further complexity. The need to tweak the formulation later does not take away from the essential divide between formulation and intervention phases.

Provided a sound and trusting therapeutic alliance has been achieved in the early sessions, the post formulation phase can go forward with a difference in tone; one that can be more robust and challenging. Once it has been agreed that this is the only way forward, ambivalence and resistance, while expected, can be met by pointing out that unless the circles are broken, the person remains stuck, the horrible feeling is given power, and the past is being kept alive in the present.

Change can be broken down into small steps, and introduced at a pace that feels manageable; which cycle to work on can be negotiated, within the limits of managing risk, but where there is no or insufficient commitment to work on change, this soon becomes apparent. The individual can be given more time by spacing out the sessions, but if even that does not work, an agreement might have to be reached that now is not the right time to engage in therapy. A letter to the client, copied to referrers if relevant, setting out clearly what would need to become negotiable for progress to be made, needs to be shared at that point. See Clarke & Nicholls (2018), p. 58 for detail on this.

Kath's goals

1   To learn to tackle both feelings and practical problems without avoiding – take the balanced approach to depression.
2   Learn to treat yourself as you would treat a good friend.
3   (Added later) Face anger and use it mindfully to give strength and courage to tackle the challenges.

Tasha's goals

1   To face the grief both about Nan's death, and about the good enough childhood that was taken from you when you were removed from Nan's home to the abuser's.
2   To allow yourself to be who you can be, fulfil your potential, accept your strengths, by treating yourself as you would a good friend.
3   (Linked) To take hold of your anger mindfully, move it from attacking yourself to owning that 'I have a right'.

Raju

While the other two were making progress, Raju was stuck in limbo. His section had been extended and medication had been forcibly administered in the form of a long-lasting injection. The initial effects of the medication were quite severe, and he was feeling shut down. He was still angry and the psychiatrist judged that he 'lacked insight'. He would not admit the need for medication or recognize that his thinking was delusional, so was liable to act on it, and therefore he needed to stay in hospital until that changed. He would not engage with the psychologist, but continued with his art work, encouraged by the OT, and he was starting to get on with one or two of the other patients on the ward. He was also forming a connection with one of the nursing assistants, who shared his Hindu faith, and with whom he talked about Hindu mythology. As there were several people on the ward with 'unshared reality', the psychologist was planning to set up a group programme to address this.

Conclusion and summary

In this chapter, the collaborative construction of the CCC formulation has been illustrated through the cases of Kath and Tasha. The emotions driving the problem behaviour have been identified, along with the immediate circumstances behind the breakdown, as well as the past issues that intensify and add to these. Kath and Tasha's strengths and potential have then been named, as this therapy deals with the whole of the person, and they will need these strengths and potential to pull them out of their stuck situation.

Only after this has been covered, are the maintaining cycles identified, with their collaboration, so that they can see that the therapist understands why they do these things; they are not bad or stupid, simply desperate. Further, they need to recognize that the behaviour is ultimately self-defeating and keeping them trapped. This is the major motivator needed to encourage someone to embark on challenging change. Once this is established, jointly owned goals for the therapy going forward can be negotiated. From now on, these will inform its direction.

In Raju's case, it was not possible to progress therapy with the psychologist, because of a rupture in the therapeutic alliance produced by events beyond her control. However, he is making cautious progress with other members of the ward team.

12 Coping skills
The basics

Introductory summary

This chapter is the first of the 'intervention'; the 'cope' as opposed to the 'comprehend', formulation, stage of the therapy. The focus here is on skills that will enable the individual to break the vicious circles that have been identified in the diagram.

The states of mind diagram (Figure 1.1), with the overlapping circles, gives the clue to the basics required to attempt the challenging changes needed to sever the maintaining cycles and break free from the grip of the horrible feeling at the heart of the diagram. Emotion mind and reasonable mind (implicational and propositional subsystems in ICS terms) work together at a medium level of arousal; when all is calm. At high and at low arousal, they become desynchronized. This leaves emotion mind, or the implicational, predominantly in charge. The result can go one of two ways. Either the individual gives in to the emotion and allows the instinctive physical reaction to take over, as when Kath lost her temper with her boss, or action is taken to block the unbearable emotion; Tasha finds self-harm will mask the unbearable feeling, for instance. Both reactions solve the short-term problem, but either way ends up with a vicious circle that reinforces the problematic emotion. In both cases, there is no conscious deliberation. Reasonable mind has left the scene, and the way is clear for emotion mind reactions, which connect directly with the body and do not refer to the conscious mind. For anything to change, the self-conscious individual needs to step in and take charge.

This leads directly to the central role of developing skills to manage both state of arousal and conscious attention. Management of attention is achieved by mindfulness, which is fundamental to the approach. Here we will look at how mindfulness is approached and used throughout the therapy, and how arousal is managed, both up and down. This will be illustrated by our three case examples.

Forging a relationship with both mind and body

Mindfulness was first introduced in Chapter 1, and in Chapter 3, its place in the development of the Third Wave CBT therapies that inform CCC was discussed. Its role in CCC has been indicated in many of the preceding chapters.

DOI: 10.4324/9781003081616-15

Volumes have been written about mindfulness, but a good place to start is the advice that comes from ACT to 'get out of your head and into your body'.

- The 'head', the thinking, chattering, self-conscious, mind, runs around between past and future, often ignoring the present. Mindfulness is about coming 100% into the present moment.
- The mind constantly sorts and sifts; it focuses attention on what it judges to be interesting; it categorises everything. Mindfulness is about letting go of judgement, bypassing categorization and sitting with whatever 'is'.
- Thoughts come and go into the mind from wherever and take over; they can become powerful. Mindfulness is about stepping back from the thoughts; noticing them without trying to block them, but being able to disengage and come back to the senses and the present moment. As DBT says: 'you are more than your thoughts'.
- The body picks up on the wayward thoughts and wheels in a stress or shutdown reaction according to their meaning for the self (the constant vigilance of the implicational for the status of the self). Mindfulness notes what the body is up to here, the little bits of tension building in certain muscles, the sinking in the stomach, etc., with detached curiosity and does not allow them power. DBT again: 'You are more than your emotions'.

In this way, patiently learning the simple but difficult practice of mindfulness means forging a new relationship between you, your mind and your body. You gain a new observer faculty.

This can then be extended out to the wider world. Ordinarily we experience the environment through the blinkers of our judgements and anticipations, and only attend to raw, sense, experience when it seems important for some reason. For instance, walking down our home street to get somewhere, ordinarily our minds would be focused on things that have just happened and things to come. Our surroundings would be familiar and not particularly interesting anyway, so we would take no notice of them, unless something different caught our eye; for instance, a new 'For Sale' notice outside a house, or a bird we could not identify. We saw in Chapter 1 how the mind is designed to notice edges and novelty.

Truly mindfully walking down the same street is a completely different experience. There is no filter, so everything is worthy of note; the feel of the foot on the tarmac, the wind on the face, the details of the houses, the clouds in the sky. In this new environment of heightened awareness, there is no space in the head for memory or anticipation. All is vividly present, and this can be quite a revelation. Go somewhere a bit more stimulating than a familiar street, say a forest, and the experience, if truly entered into, can be quite overwhelming and magical.

Mindfulness and the inner relationship

Mindfulness also introduces a change of gear in the broader relationship between us and ourselves; the 'self/self-relationship'. It is an opportunity to experience ourselves anew, no longer taking for granted the way our minds and bodies just get on with things. We are gaining new insight into the 'engine room', so to speak, and can, for instance, wonder at the way that our breathing just carries on, keeping us alive and connected with the outer world no matter what; how our bodies are designed to keep us safe, however misguided their efforts at times. All this can be observed with compassionate, possibly slightly amused, detachment, letting go of the judgements and intolerance that can characterize the usual self/self-relationship.

When introducing mindfulness to people, they often misunderstand and assume they are supposed to empty the mind of thoughts, and so declare they can't do it. They think they have failed because their focus has slipped. The teacher simply asks whether they noticed that their mind had wandered, and when the reply is affirmative, point out that it is precisely that noticing that is mindfulness. Similarly, people sometimes object: 'It didn't work this time. I didn't feel calm'. Again, the misunderstanding can be gently explained. If they felt calm last time they were mindful, that was a bonus. Mindfulness is not designed to achieve a particular goal, but rather to notice what is. If it is distress or inner turmoil that is noticed, it could be important that the individual knows about it. In this way, it is not really possible to fail at mindfulness.

Thus, mindfulness ushers in a new take on the world; a new relationship between ourselves and both our own process and the world around us. It allows us to experience the world afresh, but also to note where our thoughts and feelings are taking us and choose to change direction. It is this potential that is of most obvious relevance to therapy. It is like rebooting the computer. Things have got into some sort of a jam and you need to start afresh. Mindfulness is the way we can do that for ourselves. It enables us to open our senses and experience the world anew; 'beginner's mind' as it is known in the Buddhist teaching where mindfulness originated. 'Beginner's mind' holds the key to re-enchanting that which has become stale and banal. Finding inspiration and creativity for the new life ahead is as important for CCC as putting the past in the past.

Using mindfulness within CCC

For anyone who has encountered mindfulness in the context of spiritual practice, it will be clear that this account represents merely 'dipping a toe into the water' of a deep and extensive pool of wisdom. Within CCC, mindfulness is quite explicitly introduced as a technique. The therapist must have had sufficient practice of it, and will indeed practice it while introducing it, and will need to have brought it into their everyday life in some form in order to appreciate its power and utility. However, an extensive daily practice is not prescribed and where this position causes any conflict or confusion with more intensive uses of mindfulness, a different label can be adopted, such as grounding and awareness training. When first introducing mindfulness to individuals who might reject something with 'hippy', spiritual connotations, other descriptors can be used. 'Bringing yourself into the present'; 'grounding yourself in your senses, the physical'; are all good starting places. Once they have come to appreciate its utility, the 'm' word can be introduced.

With this introduction it remains to illustrate the application of mindfulness within CCC by showing how it was used to help Kath face the daunting prospect of giving the police details of the communications received from the stalker.

K: I … I don't think I can face doing it.

TH: I do appreciate that it feels really daunting. We need to do a mindfulness before the end of the session, and I am thinking that a mindfulness of finding your strong centre might help here. Could we give that a try and then see how you feel about it?

K: Yes, alright.

TH: Good. So see you are sat comfortably and I will start.
Turn your attention away from your thoughts to your body.
Notice how it feels.
Notice your weight on the chair.
Notice your feet on the floor.
Notice the things you normally do not notice because they are not important.
Notice judgements, gently let go of them and take in everything.
Notice the fact that you are breathing.
Notice what that feels like.
Notice your spine holding up your body.
Notice your head at the top of your spine.
Lift your head and look around, with your eyes open.
Take in what you can see.
Consider, you have a right to take your place here, now, in this moment.
Notice that you are gathered together here, in this place, in this moment.
You can watch and experience what is happening outside and within you.
You have found your strong centre – a place you can always come back to and take charge from.
From this strong centre, turn your attention to you the challenge of going to the police.
Notice how this affects you – any tension/emotion/disturbance?
Notice where you feel this in your body.
Examine the sensation with curiosity.
I am going to stop there and ask you, what do you feel now?

K: 'I have a right' feels a bit strange, but also good. When I think about the police and Ron, I feel tightness in my chest and uncomfortable in my stomach.

TH: These tensions, sensations in the gut or the chest have the power to take over your life.
Describe them to yourself in detail.
Note that these are just events in your body.
You don't need them; that sort of action is not helpful right now.

Let them go without judgement and return to noticing your breath, and what you can see, hear and feel from your strong centre.
Pause.
Let us come back to the room now. What do you think?

K: I must try and do it. I can't just carry on living in fear.

TH: That is the spirit. Do use this mindfulness to help. Hold up your head and remind yourself – you have a right to be kept safe, the same as everyone else.

Managing arousal – keeping the circles together

The other basic building block of the therapy is arousal management. This is key, as the two circles in the States of Mind diagram drift apart at high and at low arousal. Therefore, learning skills to bring down high arousal, stress, anxiety, anger, etc. and to maintain concentration and focus in the present, will ensure that wise mind can be regained where it is slipping. As 'action breathing' means breathing in more than you breath out in order to ensure there is plenty of oxygen and blood supply for vigorous activity, anyone can signal to their body that this is not required by simply breathing out more than in, and by relaxing the muscles on the out-breath. Focused activity in the present is like-wise not difficult to achieve – except that the individual might not feel inclined to engage in it. All these strategies require an act of will; motivation, and engendering this, along with hope and self-belief, are central to CCC.

Let us turn to Tasha to illustrate this.

TH: So, it seems you really recognize that these rows with your mother [*pointing to the diagram – see left hand vicious circle on Tasha's diagram*] just make things worse. You are telling me that, at the same time as being angry with her (and yourself where you have let yourself down), you realize that she has a lot to put up with, what with her health problems and the challenge of your disabled brother, to say nothing of your other two brothers. So, though it is a bit of a relief to have a go at her at the time, and she does wind you up, you would feel better if you could keep your cool, and maybe save up that useful anger to give you a sense of 'I have a right' when you need it.
Would you feel better if you could do that?

TA: Yes, but I don't think that would work. See, when she talks to me like that, I just see red!

TH: It looks as if you are getting quite tense now, just thinking about it.

TA: Yeah. I am.

TH: Like we said before, that means your body has picked up that you may be under threat so it is getting ready to fight (or run away). Any use right now?

TA: No, course not.

TH: So, let's try something to switch off that reaction. What does your breathing feel like?

TA: Quite short.

TH: Absolutely. That is action breathing – you would need to gulp in lots of air if you really were going to get into a physical fight. For now, that is not helping – it just signals to your brain to look around for threat – a guarantee that you will find it and feel even more wound up. The way to switch if off is simple. Just breathe out more than you breathe in. Can we try that?

TA: OK.

TH: (*Models the breathing and instructs*)

IN for one.

OUT – one and two.

Breathe out more than you breathe in!

And – you do not need to breathe in straight after you have breathed out – you can have a little rest.

Breathe IN – one.

OUT – one and two.

AND R-E-S-T.

As you naturally relax your chest muscles on the out-breath, it is very easy to relax your muscles on the out-breath!

Breathe IN.

AND R-E-L-A-X.

Could you follow that?

TA: Yes.

TH: How did you find it?

TA: Bit calmer now.

TH: I suggest you practise that in lots of odd moments so you get good at it. Then, what you need to try, when you get back and your mother starts needling you, just remember: the body gets ready for action, but you need to turn it off. If it is too difficult to use the breathing straight away, just leave the situation and do it elsewhere. Then come back and say something very neutral. What would that feel like?

TA: Good. It would actually show that I am more together than her which would feel good – if I can do it.

TH: Never mind if it doesn't work first time – it is never easy to do something differently. But remember, if you don't give into your anger, you are not giving it power over you. You are more in control.

Staying focused: Raju

Raju's problem is that he drifts away from consensual reality into his own world, which tends to be more attractive than the shared world for him at the moment, so that staying focused might not be very appealing. We have left him detained in hospital under a section of the Mental Health Act, forcibly medicated and angry both with the psychologist and the psychiatrist. The medication has generally shut him down, so that the ideas that were so compelling have become fuzzier. They have also become considerably more threatening and less positive. However, at one (probably not conscious) level, he does not want to give up on them as the alternative; admitting that it was all delusion and he has schizophrenia is even worse. As a result, he is not saying the right things to the psychiatrist to get him out of hospital or to reassure anyone, including Ambika, that he is safe to go home. He is stuck.

Meanwhile, he has made friends with a couple of the younger men on the ward. He has had a good conversation with the Hindu nursing assistant about mythology, and he has been getting on with the art work that the OT set him up with. All this brings him into the shared world. In the case of both the mythology conversation and the art work, there is something of a bridge to the unshared world – he is sharing it and it is communicating; he is being listened to and his art work is admired by everyone as it is actually good, even if it incorporates material from 'the other' reality.

Though he will not engage with the psychologist, he has been attending the regular mindfulness groups on the ward, set up but not run by her. Usually her assistant (who is there every day, while the psychologist is only part time on the ward) and members of the nursing team run them. Through learning mindfulness, Raju is getting the hang of waking up to the real world around him, and being able to distance himself from what is going on in his head to some extent.

Conclusion and summary

This chapter has introduced the basic skills for bringing the two parts of the mind together. Mindfulness develops an observing capacity that can notice what is going on for each without getting drawn in. Bringing down arousal through breathing, or bringing it up through concentrated activity also allows wise mind to take control. These skills facilitate the building of a new relationship between mind and body.

At this point, the individual has started to take the central role in the collaboration. The therapist can suggest things and check how they have been received. The person with mental health challenges needs to go out there and build this new relationship with their body, their self, and the world around them. Only they can break the cycles that bind them. Medication and skills can help, but from now on the person is in charge. It is up to them to take the power away from the spikey emotion at the centre of the diagram and choose to use a different coping strategy. Thus, the emotion is critical. The individual needs to develop the ability to notice the emotion creeping up, and to find the strength to stand up to it and diffuse its power. Kath needs to manage her fear of going to the police about her stalker, and Tasha, to forestall the smooth slide into a row with her mother. The prospect is daunting in both these examples. In the next chapter, the subject of managing emotions will be expanded, along with increasing the motivation necessary to pursue this goal.

13 Harnessing motivation and a new role for emotions

From problem to solution

Introductory summary

The position of the unbearable feeling at the heart of the CCC formulation diagram illustrates the way emotion has taken control of the individual and is dictating their behaviour, as shown in the maintaining cycles. Giving in to this process keeps the emotion alive, keeps the individual stuck in the emotion mind that does not understand time, and so keeps the past alive in their life. Only breaking the cycle by refusing to give into the emotion will halt this process, and with it, the reinforcement of the feeling. New skills to manage emotions are necessary to make this possible.

We have considered emotions and how to manage them in Chapter 6. However overwhelming and seemingly intractable, they can be faced, expressed healthily and let go of. To refer to the metaphor used in DBT, emotions are like a wave. If they are allowed to take their course, and allowed healthy expression they will go on their way, and the individual can face whatever challenge presents itself with the cool thinking of their wise mind. In this way, emotions can smooth the way to facing reality. However, this takes courage, and the vicious circles arise from attempts to avoid meeting the feelings head on like this. Rather than face the full force of the feeling, it is easier to brood on it, to ruminate and keep the worry or the grievance around in the mind. Alternatively, giving into them and letting the body take over and dictate the action can become the habitual way of coping, with its own built in short-term reinforcement.

The motivational message is central to preparing someone for the daunting task of managing emotions differently. The evidence of the diagram, that going round the cycle reinforces the feeling and so continues to keep the traumatic past alive in the present, is the starting point. The use of metaphor and mindfulness techniques to help Kath and Tasha manage situations that feel too daunting will be introduced in this chapter.

Working with feelings entails uncovering the hidden feeling lurking behind the more obvious emotion, and uncovering this provides a way forward for our two example cases. Kath was helped to see that buried anger lay behind her persisting depression. Similarly, Tasha's bravado hid deep hurt that she feared facing. The central message of the chapter is that once faced and uncovered like

DOI: 10.4324/9781003081616-16

this, the feelings hold within themselves the route to healing and growth. Kath's anger conceals the important message that she has the right to stick up for herself in the face of powerful people and institutions, and Tasha's relationship with her nan, which she keeps buried as it is too painful to face, carries the seeds of building a sounder relationship with herself.

Emotion and change

The formulation reveals clearly that the emotion is the engine that drives the vicious circles which keep the individual stuck in a dysfunctional way of coping. This then gets labelled as 'mental illness'. Medication can make a difference, because it dulls the emotion. Where the emotion is pushing the person into dangerous behaviours and loss of functioning, this can make sense. Medication can enable someone to find sufficient 'Wise Mind' to be able to start thinking about things and taking on new suggestions, or bring them into sufficient awareness of shared reality that there can be two way communication. However, used long term, there are diminishing returns and dependency issues, and crucially, in order to get to the root of the problem, the feeling does actually need to be faced, and if it is faced, has the potential to be the solution as well as the problem.

The challenge of facing the emotion was already seen in Tasha's case in Chapter 11. In the course of working out the diagram, it became apparent that powerful feelings about her nan are at the root of Tasha's recent relapse. The pain of being taken away from her nan, who loved and cared for her, into a household where she was abused and neglected, returns vividly to her, when she thinks about her nan, and feels too powerful and dangerous to face. It is easier to treat herself with contempt as she was treated in her mother's house.

The therapist points out that the loving and caring relationship with her nan offers the clue to her developing a caring and accepting relationship with herself. This would open up the possibility of her allowing herself to make the most of her potential, for instance in terms of her career. It could be the key to a relationship with herself that does not include self-harm and other self-destructive behaviours. Tasha can see the logic of this, but is frightened to attempt it. Matters proceed as follows:

TH: So, it is the fear of facing that hurt that stands in the way of allowing yourself to cry for your nan, and feel your sadness that you have lost her. Lost her twice in fact, both as a child and with your recent bereavement. If you could bear to feel that sadness, you could also feel the love and care she gave, which you now need to give to yourself.

TA: I just don't know what I'd do if I go there.

TH: It sounds as though that fear is thoroughly in control – like a bully that gets you to do exactly what he or she wants. Does that give you a clue? What do you have to do about a bully?

TA: Get your mates and show them you're not afraid. Bullies are usually cowards when it comes to it.

TH: So, do you see where this is heading – I am afraid I will have to do for your mates! Can we try mindfully looking at the fear as a way to start facing the bully.

TA: OK.

TH: [Goes through the usual preliminaries of grounding in the present, awareness of body, breath and surroundings.]

Now allow that fear of facing your feelings about your nan into your mind.

Note where you feel the fear in your body.

Do you feel tension in your muscles?

Sinking feeling in your stomach, etc.?

Note the way the fear takes over your body – that is what makes it powerful.

Note that the feeling is just an event in your body.

Getting your body ready for action – but is there anything to run away from or fight right now?

You do not need to follow it. Note the sensations and gently let them go. I am going to stop there and ask you what you are feeling.

TA: I feel sick. I can't breathe. My head hurts. I can't just let it go.

TH: Think about the feeling like this – what colour is it?

TA: A horrible sort of blacky-grey.

TH: Look in your mind's eye. What shape is it – can you see it?

TA: It's like some sort of monster animal; it's got claws and staring eyes – like a cat but much, much, bigger. Very fierce.

TH: Can you look into its eyes – use all your courage. Can you make it smaller?

TA: Yes. When I look into its eyes it does feel less frightening. It's getting a bit more like our black cat. He's pretty mean and scratches, but I'm not afraid of him.

TH: Let's come back now. Any thoughts? [Gets feedback. Checks risk.] Is that something you could work on before next time? If you can face the fear, you might be able to try some tears – but with something really nice to turn to afterwards. [They problem solve the treat to reward facing the ordeal.]

That mindfulness illustrates how the feeling can be broken down and, if the person has a good imagination, made more manageable. The bully image for the feeling is one of several possible ones that can be employed to motivate and enable someone see that it is in their interests to face something they have been avoiding.

Emotions that hide behind other emotions

Most spiky centres to CCC diagrams contain several emotions. Sometimes they start with just one or two, but others get added as the therapy proceeds and the underneath feelings start to emerge. An example of this from Kath's therapy follows.

TH: So, you are feeling really down and not able to do anything much this week, and you are worried that it will be the same next week when you have to go back to work. Have you got a sense of what is dragging you down?

K: I am just feeling low. My depression has come back.

TH: You have got more time to brood over things when you are not at work. What has been going on in your head?

K: There are all these worries. The way Dad treats Mum. I ought to go over there more and try and help but I just can't face the way he is – both with her and with me. Then there is Ron, who sends all these texts. Most of them are OK, but I don't want to hear from him at all, and some are really threatening in a veiled sort of way, and I sometimes see him parked down the road – yes, I know, I ought to tell the police … And of course, when I go back to work I have to face Cheryl and all her little digs and watching for me to trip up.

TH: It sounds as though you have a lot of really nasty things to contend with. I am wondering whether you feel a bit angry about some of them; your father, Ron, Cheryl? You would have a right to.

K: I really try hard not to feel angry – that would make me just like Dad. I don't want that. Angry people are horrible, and it just makes things worse if you get angry and tell people what you think of them – I nearly lost my job doing that to Cheryl.

TH: I totally agree, *getting* angry with someone, losing your temper and saying things you regret is a really bad idea. The thing is, you can use mindfulness to separate out *feeling* anger from acting on your anger. I agree that feeling anger can be unpleasant too, but in fact, anger has its uses.

K: I don't think anger is useful. I wish there wasn't such a thing.

TH: But anger is your protection. You need it so that you don't get walked over. Everyone has the capacity for anger, and if you just sit on it and try to pretend it isn't there that doesn't really work. Does that make sense?

K: I can see that could be another thing stressing me out.

TH: Precisely – you have got it. And my guess is that that stress is what is dragging you down and making you feel depressed. What do you think?

K: Yes, that is probably it. But what do I do? I don't want to be a horrible, angry person, and I have already discovered that if I let it out, it just means trouble and I feel even worse about myself.

TH: You don't need to let it out in that way. You have been practicing mindfulness, and have already shown that you can use it to stop yourself following your mood and go in a different direction – for instance, doing things when you felt depressed. Right at the beginning, when you were very anxious, I introduced to you that breathing that turns off the 'fight or flight' – that was flight. This is fight. You can bring yourself into the present moment, breath to switch the body out of action mode and make a 'Wise Mind' choice. Then you can use the wonderful resource that the anger represents!

Introducing the positive use of anger

K: Sounds a bit of a tall order, but I can see how that would help me not to lose my temper, but I would still be feeling angry.

TH: Yes, you are right. Your body will probably still be in 'action mode', and you might need to do something about that first, before you can really make use of the positive potential of the anger. The simplest way to do that is to choose something physical – give it some action. Go for a run, dig the garden, some housework – something to discharge it into. Or you can express it – you are artistic. You could make an angry picture or something. Does that give you any ideas?

K: There is always housework to do. Going for a run could be nicer, but I have to be at home for my daughter.

TH: So, if you either do the housework or the run when you get the chance, putting the energy that the anger gives you into it, the trick is not to keep on thinking about what you are angry about, but to switch to noticing how well you are running, or how you are getting the house looking good. Then you can become aware of the strength that the anger gives you and notice something else it brings with it. You would not become angry if you did not think something was wrong. That means that if you are being treated badly, some part of you is aware that you have a right to better. Does that make sense? How does that feel?

K: I hadn't thought of it like that, but now you say it, I suppose so. In the case of my mother, of course, I am thinking that she has a right, and that is easier. But with Ron and Cheryl, I guess I would not have any anger about them if I felt that what they were doing was OK. It isn't.

TH: That is really useful – can you hang onto that 'I have a right' – along with the energy the anger gives you as it gets your body ready for action. Can you feel that could give you the courage to face all the formidable challenges you have before you?

Tasha and positive use of anger

By self-harming and hating herself, Tasha is treating herself badly in the way she was badly treated by her mother and stepfather as a child. Cognitive Analytic Therapy (CAT) is very good at identifying these persistent patterns of relating, calling them 'Reciprocal Roles'. It is common to carry a reciprocal role throughout life, always relating to certain other people and yourself in ways that were learnt long before. In the case of abusive relationships such as the ones Tasha experienced, this is a dangerous pattern.

The therapist attempted to chip away at this pattern by using the anger, overt, not hidden away in Tasha's case, positively as follows:

TH: I see a lot of anger in the way you have been harming yourself over the last week.

TA: Yeah. Like I said, I hate myself and that is the best way to get the feeling out.

TH: Have you thought any more about the idea I floated last session, that by treating yourself badly, you are carrying on where the people who treated you badly as a child left off?

TA: Mmm.

TH: What about anger with them? Not suggesting you should do or say anything to them. I know you are aware of the pressure your mother is under, and there is nothing you can do about her ex – you tried and nobody backed you up. But can you just get hold of the sense that none of that should have happened; that you had a right to better?

TA: OK. But I don't see how that helps if I can't get back at them and like you say, I can't.

TH: How do you feel when you think about all that?

TA: Tense. Want to punch something.

TH: Exactly. Your body has got ready for action. Is there any action you could give it – you go to netball sometimes, don't you; what about that, that needs energy, and I know you help Mum a lot in the house – what you put that energy into doesn't matter. What does matter is moving focus from those things that happened that spark the anger, to your strength to do and achieve things now – reminding yourself that 'you have a right' is important here. (Practical ideas for discharge are explored here with Tasha.)
Another idea that a lot of people find helpful is to express the anger somehow – the simplest way is to write it down. Say all the things you would really like them to hear, but know it would just cause trouble and get nowhere if they got to see it – so it is very important to tear it up straight away afterwards. But letting yourself see it down on paper can feel quite strong. You could bring it here first and read it to me. That would make it real. Other people find doing an angry picture, writing a poem or a song lyric does the trick. Could you use any of those suggestions to shift the anger away from attacking yourself?

TA: I like the idea of the picture.

TH: Excellent – perhaps bring it along next time – and try one of the physical ways of releasing the anger as well.

Raju

In Raju's case, his relationship with feelings was not straightforward. We have already speculated about what might be going on underneath; feeling trapped in a profession he hated, while his wife's career made progress, and under pressure from his wider family to be a father and head of a household. From his perspective, he has made momentous discoveries and was on the brink of great things, but with powerful forces ranged against him. He became angry with Ambika and others who denied this reality. Worse followed: his enemies have succeeded in trapping him in hospital, labelling and medicating him, until he was no longer really sure what he thought.

It was not possible to address these emotions fully until his feet were more back on the ground, particularly as everything was immensely challenging, and there was always a danger he would retreat back into the unshared world if it got too much. He needed time to come to terms with a different perspective on things, one that was not necessarily shared by all members of the team.

Meanwhile, he was making steps towards shared reality. He was building relationships, with the OT, some staff and some other patients. His art work was both absorbing and expressive of his unshared reality, and valued in the shared world. The assistant psychologist persuaded him to meet the psychologist again, just so that she could introduce the new group they would be running together. It was called the 'What is real group' and the psychologist explained that it looked at the whole business of strange experiences and unshared ideas in a new way; one that takes them seriously, but helps people to manage them so that they do not mess up their lives. Raju was intrigued, and two of his new friends from the ward were joining, so he agreed. Raju's progress in the group will be continued in Chapter 17.

Conclusion and summary

This chapter has introduced a variety of ways of working with emotions within CCC. Some, like the mindfulness of an emotion that was introduced to Tasha to help her face her feelings about her nan, directly derive from the emotional coping skills found in DBT. Others, like the positive use of anger, are purely CCC. Motivational encouragement is an integral part of this challenging work, as the approach invariably invites the individual to go to places they have hitherto successfully ruled out and avoided.

Having introduced these strategies for coping with emotions and making positive use of feelings, this chapter brings this section to a close. We now move from 'cope' to 'connect', to consideration of relationship. In reality, there is not a hard and fast division between the two, and we have seen how facing the feelings about her nan is the key to Tasha being able to build a healthier relationship with herself. Being able to stop attacking herself through self-harm, and instead wholeheartedly embrace her potential, is emerging as a way forward for this therapy.

We now return to the notion of healing the self/self-relationship, introduced in Chapter 7. The other theme encountered at this juncture is that of the different aspects of the self, and the potential that uncovering these will have for unlocking new directions going forward. In the next section we will see how these elements of the therapy can be used to support Kath and Tasha further to achieve their goals.

Section IV

Forging new relationships: Connect

This section explores how new ways of interacting with relationship, both beyond and within the self, can be grasped using mindfulness. This is approached in a spirit of acceptance of the inherent impossibility of total control over any of these aspects of relating, and therefore a tolerance of uncertainty. Coming from that basis, relationship can be engaged with creatively in the service of growth, realising potential and pursuing valued action in the world.

DOI: 10.4324/9781003081616-17

14 Healing the relationship with the self

Introductory summary

All human beings are a relationship with themselves. Our internal dialogue reflects the nature of that relationship. People in mental health difficulties generally treat themselves badly, because that is how they feel about themselves, and it is often this bad treatment that gets labelled as symptoms of an illness. This chapter covers building a different relationship with the self, in defiance of the feeling. The actual process of doing this is illustrated from the therapies with Kath and Tasha, as this is a crucial intervention for both, and one that throws up challenges. Kath was willing enough, but it was a matter of pinning it down to actual behaviour changes. For Tasha, it proved too much of a challenge in the short term, but was a crucial step towards unlocking the emotional tangle that was impeding progress. Raju was introduced to self-compassion through a group that was part of the psychological programme available on the ward where he was detained.

Once the challenge of achieving a better self/self-relationship has been surmounted, the resulting fuller expression of the self can form a basis from which to transform relationships with others.

The context of relationship

In Chapter 4, the human being was situated firmly within a web of relationships, past and present, near and distant. These relationships, and the emotions whereby we navigate them, determine our internal state; whether it is one of calm contentment or fear and unease, for instance; they are further intimately connected to that felt sense through the constant monitoring of our place in the primate hierarchy. This is all implicational subsystem, emotion mind territory, so goes under the radar of consciousness. Unsurprisingly, old patterns of coping, based on earlier circumstances and familiar, unexamined assumptions, govern many of our patterns of relating. Such habits of relating lie behind many dysfunctional ways of coping, and resulting emotional distress; such patterns of behaviour and distress are identified by the medical system as symptoms of mental illness. Consequently, becoming aware of our relating, and exploring new ways of connecting, are central to the enterprise of escaping these traps and building a new life. In CCC, issues of

DOI: 10.4324/9781003081616-18

connection are divided three ways; the self/self-relationship; self-other; and relationship within the parts of the self. The first is the subject of this chapter.

Our relationship with ourselves

Chapter 7 introduced the idea of the self in a state of continuous evolution and repair, and the self/self-relationship as an integral part of this. How we feel about ourselves, our self-esteem, is a function of how we treat ourselves, which is in its turn influenced by how others treated us in the past and the extent to which we have been able to make positive use of this, or move beyond it where it was unhelpful. Self-compassion is therefore a key component in the tool kit towards forging a way forward that breaks free of dysfunctional patterns of behaviour, and hence free of the past. For many people, healing a damaged relationship with the self is the route to mental wellbeing.

The internal dialogue, and reflection on its content, is the way into discovering the nature of that crucial relationship. The development of a compassionate self/self-relationship is encouraged through mindfulness of self-compassion and engaging in behavioural change compatible with the new relationship, as opposed to relying on substitution of friendly for hostile content within the internal dialogue alone. It is necessary to be prepared to pursue this new relationship in the face of 'feeling', and this means working at the implicational, emotion mind, level.

Mindfulness of self-compassion is a powerful tool as it activates the 'soothing, safeness' state introduced with Gilbert's (2005) work on compassion, discussed in Chapter 7. This state is activated during the mindfulness by bringing to mind a compassionate, caring relationship. This can be with another human being, usually a child or someone in need of care, or it might be a pet animal. Once this relationship is alive in the imagination, the individual is instructed to really notice the effect that this has on the body and the mind. The challenge is then to transfer this safe, soothing state to the relationship with the self.

Characteristically, this encounters resistance, based on its feeling false, undeserved, etc. The counter argument here is that the old self/self-relationship will have been driven by self-hatred and worse, which will have stunted confidence and achievement and so reinforced the grounds for self-denigration. The only way to break out of this cycle is to act 'as if' one was one's own good friend, intent on promoting their best interests. As well as the obvious self-care and bringing enjoyable activity into life, the true friend will be prepared to challenge, but in an understanding, not in a harsh way. This is the 'honest' friend who counters the 'false' friend. The false friend advocates the easy way out, which usually lands up in a vicious cycle based on avoidance of emotion. This work can prove challenging, as we have already begun to see in the case of Tasha. Kath had already laid the foundations cognitively in her previous therapy, when she learnt to challenge self-critical thoughts, giving grounds for more optimism in her case.

Kath

As already indicated, Kath could see the point of treating herself better even when she struggled to actually do it, and the mindfulness of self-compassion was important in giving her an emotional grasp of what she was aiming at. The caring relationship she chose to focus on was that with her daughter, Lily, to whom she had essentially devoted her life. We pick up the session at the point of the reflection following the mindfulness.

TH: Tell me what you noticed.

K: I can see the point of it, but it was difficult. I really got in touch with wanting to care for and protect my daughter. It drew tears when I sensed how much I love her. It was a lovely warm feeling, but with a bit of anxiety in the sto- mach, as I know I cannot always be there and protect her, and that will get more difficult as she gets older. Turning that to myself felt really strange and wrong, but I think I managed it a little bit.

TH: That sounds good and also honest. Maybe something you can work on. Tell me more about what got in the way.

K: It just felt selfish – I need to give everything to her. She only has me, so she is really dependent on me.

TH: I can see that is real, and a big responsibility. What will make you best able to shoulder that responsibility?

K: What do you mean? Do you mean about my mental health?

TH: Exactly. It sounds like you got in touch with the necessity to be strong in order to be there for her. What will help you to be that strong?

K: I suppose that is about me looking after myself, even if it does feel weird. If I didn't get so anxious and depressed, she would be happy. However hard I try to hide what is going on, I know she worries about me when I am down, and she shouldn't have to at her age, should she?

TH: Absolutely. That is a good place to start. But for it to really work, you have got to do it for you as well – after all, your daughter won't need you in the same way as she gets older. That will change, but you have a life to live, and as you can see, looking at your strengths on the diagram, there is a lot there to develop. How can you get started treating yourself as a good friend? What would you do differently?

K: What do you mean?

TH: Imagine you had a friend in trouble, under the sorts of pressure that you are under, who had come to stay, and you wanted to help her get back on her feet. What would you do?

K: I would let her talk about it. Maybe go somewhere nice to take her mind off it. Cook her nice food … is that what you mean?

TH: Exactly! You have got it. What about doing that for you?

K: Well, I can't exactly talk to myself, and it's not much fun going places on your own. As for cooking, I make what Lily will eat, which is not usually my first choice.

TH: I seem to remember you saying earlier that one of the things you had been avoiding was getting in touch with friends. If you tried a few, maybe you could find someone to go out with – or indeed, you could try something you would enjoy but just with Lily. As for the cooking – I am sure your internal good friend could try and tempt you with something you like, that you could make just for you, along with the fish fingers or whatever it is that Lily will eat?

K: It feels really scary to phone my friends – they tried to keep in touch with me, but I kept putting them off, so I feel really bad, and they have by and large given up by now. It has been so long.

TH: Can we make a plan for a couple of things to do before next time? Can you think of the friend it would be easiest to start with?

K: Yes, there is one. We used to do a lot together.

TH: Right. You need to phone her and just have a conversation. You don't need to make it heavy. Commit to a time. Stick to it, using breathing and mindfulness to manage the anxiety and reluctance. You also need to plan to buy and cook one thing that you like this week. Can you give that a go and report back? No worries if it is too difficult, but it would be a great start to getting your internal good friend up and running.

Next session, Kath had not done anything about the cooking, but she had managed to phone the friend, who was delighted to hear from her, and they agreed to meet up. This proved doubly helpful as it gave her a sympathetic but realistic perspective on her various challenges, where Kath could be persuaded to share them. For Kath, conjuring up and consulting her internal good friend was a powerful tool for change. The good friends – real and imaginary, both encouraged her to care for herself and to tackle difficult challenges in a sensible, measured, manner.

Tasha

With Tasha, things did not run so smoothly. From the start, she had declared that she hated herself, and that the self-harm, as well as being the most effective way of numbing intolerable feelings, felt like justified punishment. The first time the mindfulness of self-compassion was introduced, it went badly. Tasha struggled to choose the object to arouse her compassion towards. There was her brother, but her feelings towards him were mixed; there was a kitten she had been very fond of and nursed, but then it died, so that was distressing. The therapist concluded that, fundamentally, she did not want to go there.

The therapist had more success in mobilizing her pride in achievement, both actual and potential, and spent quite a lot of time dwelling on her potential as represented on the strengths bow on the diagram. The college tutor who was encouraging her to work towards a nursing degree proved the 'good friend' in this instance. The fact that her abilities were being recognized here appealed to the defiant side of Tasha in a way that being nice to herself did not. Tasha agreed to pursue this, and acknowledged that in order to do so, she would have to work to curb the urge to harm herself, as she could see that such behaviour was not compatible with this ambition.

Things seemed to be on track, but then Tasha started to miss sessions. For the first couple she gave half plausible excuses. Then she simply failed to turn up. The therapist tried phoning and texting without avail. It got to the point where she needed to send the letter discharging her if she continued to fail to make contact.

Raju

The group programme in the hospital included a 'Compassionate Friend' group, which covered the principles of the good friend and the honest friend (see Chapter 7). This was organized by the psychology department, and facilitation was shared between the assistant psychologist, the OT department and interested nurses when they could be spared. Raju was a quiet member of the group, but when partici-pants were split into pairs, helping each other to find the 'good friend' challenge to the critical internal dialogue, Raju found both that it was easier to identify this for others, and that his own attitude to himself was heavily influenced by the messages he had received throughout his life from his father and brothers. His partner in the group helped him to recognize that although he had always rebelled against them to an extent, in another way he had accepted that he was inferior because he could not match their hard-headed business mentality. She was quite indignant when Raju recalled how his brothers, in particular, had ridiculed him and put him down, and he could begin to see how that had impacted on the way he related to himself. Discussing this further in a session with the psychologist later, he was able to acknowledge that his talents lay in directions they did not comprehend, and the positive evidence of his potential, his achievements in art and mathematics, had been overshadowed by the weight of disappointed expectations. Now was the time to start to own what he could do as opposed to what he could not, by developing a more encouraging internal dialogue.

Conclusion and summary

This chapter has opened the 'connect' section of the CCC course of therapy, by illustrating working on the self/self-relationship. There are a number of stages to this work. Recognizing the existence of the internal dialogue and the revelation of its nature and content is the first. Tasha and Kath had achieved that, but Raju was just beginning to become aware of it.

The next stage is to bring this internal relationship to life as something sepa-rate. The role of mindfulness to create a detached, observing position is crucial here. Next, it is necessary to appraise, in an objective manner, the effect that a critical, bullying relationship has on the person and their ability to take risks and try out new things. The group that Raju attended covered this through a lively discussion.

The contrasting relationship with the good friend, someone you want to take care of and do your best by, needs to be brought to life next. This was managed in Kath's case by the mindfulness of self-compassion, and in Raju's, through the pair work in the group. Tasha has not yet managed to get to that point.

Next comes the challenge of turning that caring towards the self. This instruction is usually experienced as alien and near impossible. The therapy with Kath illustrates how this new insight needs to be translated into specific behaviour change to become embedded. Faced with a good friend in trouble, you would want to do something to help. The same applies to the internal relationship, and underlines the concrete, behavioural, nature of the intervention stage of the therapy.

As if managing the relationship with oneself were not complicated enough, all this is embedded in a world of relationships with other people, impinging on the process in ways that are even more difficult to predict and affect directly than the self/self-relationship. It is to managing relationships with important others that we turn in the next chapter.

15 Relationships with other people
Unravelling the tangles

Introductory summary

This chapter examines the different ways in which relationships with others can be distorted by 'spiky' feelings and the legacy of the past, and suggests CCC ways in which these can be addressed, with the help of the clinical cases.

The intrinsic uncertainty inevitable in a real relationship with another human being creates huge anxiety for those who have been badly hurt in the past, so do not want to risk making themselves vulnerable again. However, human beings need relationship, and there are a number of ways in which people try to circumvent that uncertainty. These are enumerated here and illustrated from the case examples. These strategies provide a spurious sense of certainty in the short term, but prevent sound and deep relationships, of the sort that will support true growth, in the longer term. The task of the therapy is to identify distorted patterns of relating, addressing the historical emotional hurts that keep people lonely or attract them to harmful or exploitative relationships, and then encourage the very real risk of entering into authentic relationship, both managing the fear that holds them back, and retaining the Wise Mind judgement that can alone ensure their safety.

The power of relationships, within and across time

Even if rebalancing the self/self-relationship is successfully accomplished, other people remain a problem and a conundrum. As described in Chapter 4, emotions manage relationships, and when the emotional part of the mind is in charge, these feelings, the spiky bit in the middle of the diagram, can start to take over. The three clinical cases illustrate in different ways how important relationships can dominate lives across time; Kath's difficult relationship with her father is reflected in her choice of partners, as well as remaining a problem in the present; Tasha struggles with the contradictory and toxic legacy of having an inadequate parental figure suddenly replace a good one, followed by sexual abuse, and Raju's life is dominated by the unmeetable expectations of his father and brothers.

Also, dealing with real people with all their complexity and their demands upon the individual can be taxing for the strongest. Those who have learnt to

DOI: 10.4324/9781003081616-19

see themselves as inferior or less entitled will find it hardest, because, below the radar of consciousness, they will have picked up that they are at the bottom of the primate hierarchy and had better not compete or else. Where people have experienced close relationships as dangerous and damaging in the past, it is unsurprising if they continue to avoid intimacy.

All these factors lead to fear and avoidance. Faced with fear, it is natural for people to seek guarantees and safety, in an area where uncertainty is the norm. There are a number of common tangles that result from efforts to negotiate relationships while by-passing the uncertain adventure of really connecting with others.

Assumptions

Because other people are inherently unpredictable, the temptation is to operate on the basis of unchecked assumptions and anticipation. This is immediately attractive because of the spurious sense of certainty and safety it appears to offer. The alternative is really interacting: being open with people and attempting to establish where they are actually coming from. This inevitably entails vulnerability, and for those who have been hurt badly in the past, that can feel just too dangerous.

Example: Kath assumed that the police would not believe her and would perhaps blame her if she complained about the stalker, and so accepted that she needed to live in fear. The solution in Kath's case was to approach the police, with encouragement from others, and discover that they did take the veiled threats and surveillance seriously, and so warned the stalker. This frightened him, as he could see the potential seriousness of a charge, and stopped his shadowing and texting.

Repeating the past

People whose early connections have been problematic can find themselves replicating their past experiences in a string of unsatisfactory relationships.

Example: Tasha's experience of men in her childhood had been one of abandonment and abuse. Unsurprisingly, boyfriends were fleeting and undesirable. When invited to reflect on this in therapy, she acknowledged that she went for the buzz of the bad boys, but then quickly extricated herself when they tried to control or exploit her. One 'good' boy had been quietly pursuing her, offering friendship and support (he had a car and was a useful source of lifts), but whenever he tried to move things into a more intimate direction, she scornfully rejected him, because he was 'boring'. One may assume that there was also an unacknowledged fear that if she let him became important to her, she would become vulnerable to the pain of another abandonment.

Giving care in order to get care

Where someone's past relationships have not given them the confidence that they are loveable or deserving of care, they will frequently take on the role of carer, based on the idea that this will elicit care in return. The assumption here is that, if they do everything possible for that individual, this will be reciprocated and they will be cared for. Unfortunately, the other person frequently fails to see it that way; they take what is offered, becoming more demanding as the other becomes more ready to give, and do not fall into the role that is expected of them but never made explicit – unless it all comes out in a major row.

Example: Kath's experience growing up was that she was unimportant and undeserving of love. Her father was cold and critical, and though her mother did love her, she was too subjugated herself to be able to be really there for her, and never dared to stand up for her in the face of her husband's hostility to his daughter. As a result, when Kath started to explore relationships in her late teens, whereas she saw securing a relationship as a desperately needed escape route from home, she had no confidence that she could be loved simply for who she was. Consequently, she made a beeline for a man with obvious problems as it seemed to her she could make herself indispensable by helping him, and be repaid with his love. This will not have been a conscious calculation but more a strategy driven by desperation. In her marriage, he took advantage of this and became more and more controlling and abusive, leading to her escape (which took courage). After a decade or so of avoiding relationships, she fell into exactly the same trap with the stalker; a needy individual on whom she took pity, until she could see the relationship heading down the same road as before, and abruptly ended it.

Problems with 'mentalizing' – or putting yourself in the other person's shoes

'Mentalizing' or mentally identifying accurately where the other person is coming from is seen as the crucial skill in Bateman & Fonagy's (2004) Mentalization-Based Treatment (MBT) for mental health, particularly aimed at the population who attract the diagnosis of personality disorder because of their difficulties with relationships. Mentalization is a sophisticated skill that requires a command of 'Wise Mind'. Where emotions take over, assumptions rule, but equally, if emotions are excluded, empathy becomes out of reach, so that reasonable mind alone is just as incapable of reaching into the mind of another.

In a CCC therapy, familiarity with the spiky diagram provides a way into developing this awareness. It makes sense to someone who has learnt to understand their problems in this way that the other person also has a spiky centre, and where their reactions appear unreasonable or unfair, they are probably driven by their 'spike'. The emotions in the spike in turn arise from current external circumstances and past hurts, independent of the person bearing the brunt of the reaction. For some, this can open up a whole new dimension.

However, some people are much *too* sensitive to where the other person is coming from and their needs and wishes. This tends to be the case with those who see caring for others as their only route to care for themselves. As we have seen, in order to break this unhelpful behavioural pattern, they need to attend to themselves first, and be able to protect themselves against being taken advantage of. This is particularly difficult where they are up against people who are persistently unreasonable and demanding.

An example here is Kath's situation with her parents. She finds the suffering of her mother, who has to contend both with her own dementia and her husband's bullying and impatience, unbearable. Her father expects help from her with the burden of caring, not taking account of all her responsibilities, but refuses to consider bringing in professional carers on grounds of cost. Kath here needs both more effective assertiveness, and the skill to accept an unresolvable situation. One aspect of this complex situation that the therapist helps her to let go of is her ongoing indignation at her father's unreasonableness. Kath was able to see, when it was pointed out, that his behaviour is not news; he has been like this all her life, so that outrage is surely redundant. The therapist suggested that Kath view him as a character in a soap opera. Whenever he comes out with something out of order, this is just his character's signature, and she can imagine the audience nodding and laughing at the predictability of it.

Fear of closeness

An understandable problem for those who have been hurt in close relationships in the past is fear of getting close to people; fear of intimacy. Intimacy means venturing deep into emotion mind, leaving the safety of the bounded self behind. This is the place where past and present merge, so, where the experience from the past has been of hurt and abuse, rejection and abandonment, it is only natural to draw back from allowing that to happen again, whenever vulnerability threatens.

This can mean avoidance of close relationships altogether. Kath spent about ten years without allowing anyone close following her escape from her marriage. Tasha keeps men at arm's length by confining herself to brief flings with men she has no intention of letting into her life. Other people will allow someone to get close at first, but when it starts to become serious, it also starts to feel scary. The reaction then is to draw back, go cold or test the person, half expecting them to turn abusive, so goading them to see when it will happen – or push them away in other ways. It feels safer to reject them before they reject you.

Because it feels so acutely dangerous, it can be hard to persuade someone to switch from avoidance to approach in this area. This was a challenge that the therapist explored with Kath, as follows.

TH: You are ruling out ever risking a relationship with a man again. I am wondering whether that isn't a bit drastic. I can appreciate that you would not consider dating, because of how unsafe it feels, but I am wondering whether this fear of closeness affects your friendships as well? How much do you feel able to open up with your friends?

K: I try not to say too much. I prefer to let them do the talking. I am a good listener.

TH: That is interesting. What is that about?

K: It doesn't feel comfortable to say too much about my stuff.

TH: Does that ever lead to a lack of balance; them doing most of the talking, so that you know more about what is going on for them than they know about you?

K: Yes, it can be a bit like that.

TH: I know from what you have said before that you tend to feel unconfident in friendships, while there is evidence that your friends want to stick by you, you don't always make it easy for them. I am wondering whether what we have just been talking about is a bit of a clue. Friendships get deeper when people share more, and this feels safest when they keep in step. If it is one-sided on either side it can feel a bit uncomfortable or not right. The friend who talks on and on and is not interested in what you have to say is of course not good company, but there can be a problem with the opposite. You find out all about them, but are reluctant to open up yourself. Can you see how that might feel?

K: Put like that, I can see it might feel a bit unfair – if they are risking telling me things and I hold back.

TH: You have put your finger on it. How would it be to try and be a bit more forthcoming next time you meet up with your friend, now that you have made the effort and renewed contact?

K: I could try. It feels a bit scary thinking about it. I have got so much going on that is not good, so it feels really uncomfortable to think about talking about it.

TH: That uncomfortable feeling could be the clue that this is something you really do need to address. If you got better at being open with your friends, that could be an important first step towards possibly reconsidering other relationships in the future. That fear that gets in the way – I am going to suggest that we use a mindfulness of emotion now to examine it.

This is an example of approaching a really sensitive area gradually, and also, the way in which mindfulness can be brought in to address, and essentially deconstruct, the feeling that is getting in the way.

The balancing act of relating

These complexities are nicely summed up in the Relationship Triangle, which is part of the DBT skills programme (Linehan 1993, p. 115). In the examples cited above, a failure of assertiveness is frequently the issue. Kath is a case in point here. However, simply concentrating on getting what you want in the short term is not always the best strategy, and DBT identifies three elements that need to be taken into consideration when approaching relationships with others. Getting what you want out of the interaction, assertiveness, is certainly one. However, where this is pursued at the expense of the relationship and its continuation, where this relationship is valued and important, it might need to be tempered. The third important aspect, which can easily get forgotten, is attending to the relationship with oneself – keeping one's self-respect in the interaction. This often gets sacrificed where someone strives to preserve the relationship with another who is bullying and exploitative.

In Tasha's case, getting these factors in balance proved particularly challenging.

Tasha and her mother

The therapist managed to get an answer from Tasha to a particularly pleading text where she expressed her concern about the missed appointments, and desire to help, and Tasha returned to therapy, but in a negative frame of mind.

T: I know you are trying your best, but it just isn't working. I have got BPD and that's it. Talking about the past and all just stirs things up.

TH: I do realize how hard it is to look at things like your feelings about your nan and what a lot of courage it takes. However, it seemed before that it was worth it as those feelings were driving your self-harm, and you really needed to be able to get a handle on that to pursue nursing.

T: Well, you can forget that! Mum hit the roof. Getting unrealistic ideas; how was she going to manage if I was working all hours and not able to claim benefits? She needs me around to help with my brothers, does Mum. College is just part time, and the family needs my PIP to get by. I can see her point.

TH: I do see that puts a lot of pressure on you, and you really are useful in your family, and don't want to let your mum down. However, my memory is that your view of all this can shift. You don't always feel like that. Sometimes you feel resentful about Mum and do want to pursue your own future. It all sounds like a bit of a tangle to me.

T: Yeah, well. I'm not that happy about it, but what do I do?

TH: It is common enough for relationships to get into this sort of a tangle, and because of that we have got a diagram here to help sort it out at least in your mind – so that you can be clear where you want to put your effort.

(Tasha and the therapist work together to fill in the three sections of the diagram (Figure 15.1): the need to keep Mum on side, and what Tasha might want out of life were relatively straightforward. The idea of Tasha keeping her self-respect, being true to herself took a bit more discussion, but she was able to see that simply falling in with what everyone else wanted would result in her feeling somehow cheated.)

T: I think I feel even worse now. I don't know what to do.

TH: One way forward would be to invite your mother to a three-way session. What do you think about that? Do you think she would come?

T: I don't know. I think she's pretty fed up with you, but she might want to come and put her side. I can ask her. And yeah, it could be I won't always want to give up on the nursing and stuff. Sometimes I just want to walk away from them all – but where would I go? And they do need me.

The session with Tasha's mother was hard work, but did move things on. Her mother started off belligerently, as predicted. As she was given space to put her side of things, more complex feelings came out: jealousy of Nan, her own mother, whom Tasha clearly preferred, and the chaos of her own life and relationships. Her own resulting thwarted ambitions led to ambivalence about

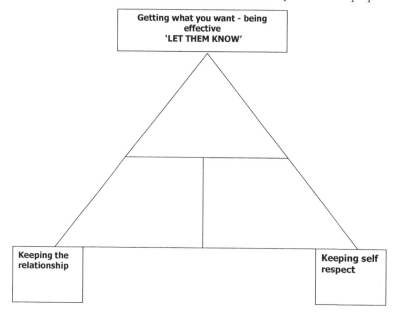

What are your priorities in this situation?

Figure 15.1 The Relationship Triangle

whether she wanted to deny her daughter opportunities she did not have, or encourage her to take them and be able to enjoy her success vicariously. Unspoken but evident were the financial and practical implications of having Tasha at home and on benefits.

In the next session the therapist built on this foundation by inviting Tasha to speculate about her mother's spiky centre. She was able to recognize its complexity, added to the fact that her mother was now more encouraging, having been given an opportunity to voice her side of it. The result was the therapy back on track to an extent, but it still felt precarious. The therapist felt as if she was floundering and not sure where it was going, concerns which she brought to supervision. The supervisor suggested directing focus towards the warring aspects within Tasha herself – leading onto the subject of the next chapter.

Conclusion and summary

This chapter has enumerated and explored the many pitfalls attendant upon risking relationship with other human beings. The account has been illustrated by the experience of two people with mental health diagnoses, and particularly unpromising relationship histories. However, these sorts of patterns and dilemma are common enough in social life in general, or else the fairy tale ending 'they lived happily ever after' would not raise the customary hollow laugh. Everybody needs to be aware of the temptation to try to secure certainty in the uncertain arena of human relations, and to notice the way in which this futile endeavour may be attempted. Forging deep, reciprocal relationships, characterized by compassion and honesty, is thoroughly worthwhile, but not easy. There will always be that balancing act between tolerance of the failings of the other and protecting one's own integrity, as human beings inevitably fall short of the ideal.

Underneath the vagaries of relating to other people lies the complexity of relationships within the self, the shifting sands. We have already covered the self/self-relationship. It is now time to tackle the relationship between the different aspects and potentials within the individual in more depth, with the help of Kath and Tasha. This will be the subject of the next chapter.

16 Aspects of self and putting the past in the past

Introductory summary

This chapter illustrates the process of identifying and naming the different aspects of their self. Continuing the ideas introduced in Chapter 7, each aspect has a positive side and one that needs to be inhibited. None is to be rejected and none uncritically adopted. Once the aspects have been identified, mindfulness can be used to navigate the way through. This work can be useful for identifying sources of stuckness and freeing the individual's unrealized potential.

Inevitably, the past is woven into these aspects as they span past internalized relationships, present survival and future potential. In order to be able to move on freely into that future, a healthy relationship with the past needs to be forged; one that takes forward what is good and makes positive use of emotions to let go of aspects that intrude into the present, as with flashbacks; or simply drag the individual backwards, as with shame, bitterness and regret.

Return to the elusive self

The theme of a fluid self, reactive to roles, relationships and circumstances, both external, and internal in the sense of past experience, has been developed throughout the book so far. From the perspective of our individual self-consciousness, we can feel coherent and in control. This feeling masks our dependence on those relationships, external and internalized from the past, that are part of our make-up. I am writing this during the COVID-19 pandemic, which has over-thrown structures of jobs and security for many, and has placed unaccustomed strains on relationships. People talk of a resulting mental health crisis. This can be seen in another way: the crisis resulting from the pandemic has shed light on the dependence that we all have on those structures that enable us to operate effectively in the world. Suddenly everything that was taken for granted changes, and our common underlying vulnerability is revealed. We are faced more sharply with the universal reality of our mortality. Further, our reliance on the complex economic and social web that holds our lives together, normally unnoticed in the background, is laid bare.

Many people, faced with this crisis, have actually found they have reserves and talents that were underutilized or previously unrealized – baking,

DOI: 10.4324/9781003081616-20

gardening and mask making come to mind. In a more general way, CCC takes advantage of this mutability of the human self in the service of growth and development. The old ways of managing that led to stuckness and distress need to be replaced by the nurturing of forgotten parts of the self, giving permission to aspects that have been squashed, while keeping other aspects, which have presumed to take over and speak for the whole, in their place among the rest and only speaking in turn. Each aspect has a positive potential and each has tendencies to be curbed. They just need managing.

This would be easy if there was a CEO to take charge; a ready-made super-self who could be summoned up. As already discussed, ICS gives us the crucial insight that there is no such boss. Control passes backwards and forward between the subsystems of our brains. Only mindfulness can give us fleeting insight into what is going on and some hope of steering it. This is not like driving a car, it is more like conducting an orchestra, made up of autonomous musicians who might have their own ideas about how the piece should sound, but who are all expert performers on their chosen instruments, so can make unique contribution to a harmonious whole, when skilfully conducted.

This is not the generally assumed picture of the self. The problem with the idea that there is a potential CEO who can be discovered and handed the power is that this opens the door to a single aspect of the self taking over, excluding or subordinating the rest, and presuming to talk for the whole. This is at best limiting and at worst dangerous, where, for instance, a very depressed or suicidal aspect grabs the helm. That is why understanding and being prepared to work with the inherent uncertainty and instability of this perspective on the self is important.

Working with aspects of self: Kath

Discussing 'aspects of self' with Kath, the therapist and Kath together immediately identified and named the most obvious one as 'Dutiful Kath'. Devotion to her daughter appeared centre stage, but she clearly felt the same way towards her mother, though her ability to give her mother the care she wanted was hampered by her father's presence on the scene. On the positive side, this placed Kath squarely as a loyal and caring individual. On the negative, it tended to mean the total subordination of her own interests and aspirations. By the time this session of the therapy was reached, Kath could acknowledge that this subordination of her interests probably played a big part in keeping her trapped and, consequently, underlaid her persistent depression. This provided impetus to look beyond that caring aspect. However, she found it hard to identify anything else for herself. The therapist probed as follows:

TH: What about your job? Despite your sickness record, they clearly value you, so you must be doing something right. Also, you have said, you have been there a long time while others come and go. I know you find it difficult to explore this, but what makes you good at your job?

K: I think I manage to click with people, even stroppy ones. I kind of get where they are coming from and they sense that.

TH: Sounds as though you are a skilful empathizer. Would that do as our second aspect?

K: Yes. I suppose that fits.

TH: The upside of that aspect is obvious, and it is a transferable skill that could take you into other areas if you ever chose to branch out. What is the downside?

K: I take on other people's stuff too much. That gets me down.

TH: Excellent. We have got aspect number two. What about number three?

K: I don't know. That just about covers my life at the moment.

TH: 'At the moment' is the clue. We need to look beyond the moment, at the things you used to do and might develop in the future. Let's look at what we have got on the strengths on your spiky diagram. [reads] 'Conscientious mother. Good at her job. Caring. Courage to leave unsuitable relationships. Made a good home for her and her daughter – good taste, artistic leanings. Loves animals and nature. Sense of spiritual connection through nature.' What about the artistic, nature loving Kath?

K: I think the artistic bit is pushing it. I just said I liked making the home look nice. But, yes, nature and animals are important for me. Since being signed off work – and since us talking about using mindfulness out of doors, I am starting to spend more time in the woods and fields near where we live, and to take photos. I do feel different when I am there – I can get quite lost in it. I got a good photo of some hares the other day, because I had been still such a long time, they didn't notice me.

TH: It does sound as though that is another aspect; one that is only just peeping out, but could be developed. What shall we call her?

The session continued with a discussion about a potential aspect around Kath as a partner. Currently, she could not see that at all, given recent experiences, but recognized that it might be one for the future.

Tasha's aspects

In Tasha's case, it was easier to identify different and even contradictory aspects and the session went well. Tasha started by saying she was 'trouble'. That gave the clue to the first aspect to be worked up, and 'Sassy Tasha' was agreed on as a name for her. Sassy Tasha was indeed mouthy, got into trouble and risky situations, and could let herself down while this aspect was in charge. It also represented her spirited side. This drew in other people, and she could be a good leader, particularly when pursuing issues of justice. She felt strongly that her disabled brother was not given the support he was entitled to, and she had played a prominent role in campaigning for a better deal for people with disabilities in her college, for instance.

Another aspect that fell out naturally they named 'Little Mother'. This captured her role in caring for her younger brothers, particularly the learning disabled one, and her protective stance towards her own mother. This aspect had clear positives, and indeed had potential to be built on to form a substantial career. On the downside, it led to the sacrifice of her own needs and interests. If it was in charge too long, Sassy Tasha got restive and caused mischief.

The therapist then brought up the self-destructive aspect that hated and actively attacked herself. Finding the positive here was the challenge, but together they were able to acknowledge that it had represented her survival strategy when her world collapsed around her. It had enabled child Tasha to manage what was happening to her and come through to the person she was now with the positive potential that had been identified. They named it 'Destroyer/Protector'.

At this point, the exploration seemed to have ground to a halt, but there is space for four aspects on the form. The session proceeded as follows:

TH: What about another aspect. It can be something that you could be – something you want to develop or have been in the past and could be picked up again?

TA: I think we've got everything there. That looks like me!

TH: I am wondering. What were you like when you were really young – before you moved back to Mum's? Can you remember that?

TA: Yeah. I was different. I was very quiet, but I was doing really well at school – they were always praising me and putting my work up on the wall. Nan was dead proud of me.

TH: That does fit in with college encouraging you, but otherwise it sounds different. Tell me more about that.

TA: It just feels horrible to think about it. I let Nan down so much.

TH: I do see that this is really difficult to talk about, but I think it could be very important.

TA: It's just that I didn't see much of Nan after, as she lived a long way away and had to take the train – also, she and Mum really didn't get on, but when she did come and saw how I'd changed, it felt dreadful.

TH: I can see that you would have changed because of what you were going through.

TA: I think Mum quite liked saying all the trouble I had been getting into at school and that. The worst was when I was 13. I'd been messing around with boys and had got an infection so had to go to that clinic, and that was just when Nan was visiting. I think she was shocked. She said [cries], 'What has happened to my good girl?'

TH: It sounds as though that was really painful – really got to you.

TA: She cared. Mum yelled at me, but I don't think she expected any different. I just felt so ashamed.

TH: Shame is a really unbearable feeling. I can see why you don't want to think about it. But can you see, this could be a clue to an important aspect of you that has been buried all this time – one that does believe in you like your nan did; one that can be successful and have self-respect. But I do see that in order to go there, we will need to do some tough work on the shame.

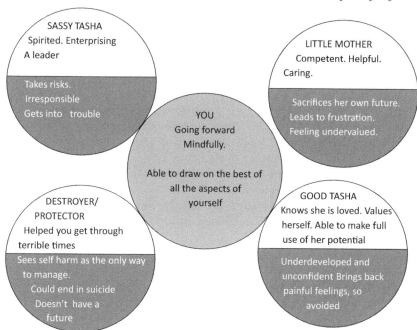

Figure 16.1 Tasha's Aspects

Building a new relationship with the past

It was clear to the therapist that Nan had believed in Tasha in a way that nobody had since (with the exception of the tutor at college), and she needed to be able to take that on as self-belief, but was prevented from doing so by her conflicted feelings. This was addressed as follows:

TH: Something to think about. We have seen how emotions don't take any notice of time – that means you can feel terrible feelings that really belong years ago when you were little as if they belonged to now. Love is a feeling too. Your nan truly loved you and you loved her. No one can take that away from you. You can still feel that if you let yourself. My sense is that it is the shame that gets in the way.

TA: That is all very well. I still feel dreadful when I think about all the hopes Nan had for me and then how it turned out.

TH: We have already looked at how you can use anger to let you feel that you have a right and to give you courage to own that. Sometimes you are really good at that. Sassy Tasha can do that. Then we looked at how the anger can help you put the past in the past and you drew that amazing picture, with speech bubbles saying what you wanted to them.

TA: Yeah. I put down what I wanted to say to them, but can't 'cos as you explained, they just won't see it like that and we will just end up shouting. It felt sort of real when I did that. He said it was my fault. I led him on. But I can see now that eight-year-olds aren't like that. Sometimes I am not sure, but I can sort of get that.

TH: That sounds like progress. The next bit is to return to self-compassion. I know that really didn't work for you before, but we have moved on now. If you knew a little girl now who went through what you went through – had to leave a loving home and be sent somewhere where she was abused – how would you act towards her?

TA: I would want to get her out of there! I'd want to tell her, they are monsters, don't listen to them, you are alright.

TH: It sounds as though you have got exactly what you need to tell little Tasha. Could we try that mindfulness again and see if it works better?

In subsequent sessions, as well as targeting the shame with mindfulness of self-compassion, the therapist was able to link this with the theme of using anger positively to view the past in a different light. This enabled Tasha to see how she behaved when she moved to her mother's as her only way of managing in an impossible situation. It was also understandable that it hurt her nan deeply to see her changed like that. Getting hold of the sense of entitlement was important in allowing Tasha to forgive herself for having let both herself and her nan down.

All this was enabling Tasha to both own her past, and to move on from it. Interestingly, this did not include exploring it, and there was relatively little attention paid to the actual abuse. This was because the live emotion seemed to centre around Tasha's relations with her nan and her mum. The therapist discussed with her that she might in the future want to pursue a therapy that focused on 're-living' – processing the abuse thoroughly in the present. Tasha was not keen on this idea, but acknowledged it could be something to think about if the past continued to present problems. For the time being, putting the past behind her with a sounder relationship to it and pursing her potential going forward was sufficient.

Return to 'Good Tasha'

Once that part of the work had been completed, the therapy returned to the aspects of self, and the task of welcoming 'Good Tasha' into the group and fitting her in. At first, Tasha assumed that the therapist would simply want her to 'become' Good Tasha. Having pointed out that all aspects have a downside, they worked out what this was in the case of Good Tasha, and identified that she was hopeless at defending Tasha from harm, and lacked the spirited qualities that were the preserve of Sassy Tasha. Tasha was able to see that she needed not to 'become' one of the aspects, but to draw on the parts that were needed as and when appropriate. A combination between the spirit and leadership qualities of Sassy Tasha, the caring skills of 'Little Mother' and the diligence in study of 'Good Tasha' would be an unbeatable combination when it came to pursuing a career in nursing! In order to get these working together, she would need to keep some of the downsides of these aspects in check, to say nothing of reining in the 'Destroyer/Protector'.

Using mindfulness to navigate something as complex as this is not straightforward, and CCC uses metaphor to help people get an emotion mind, felt sense, of what they are supposed to be doing. The usual metaphor for managing the aspects of self is the orchestra conductor, but the therapist recognized that Tasha was unlikely to have ever experienced an orchestra. She hit on managing an unruly bunch of children while trying to get on with something else. The aim in using mindfulness to manage aspects of self is to develop a background awareness of what is going on; which aspect is in charge? Are they taking over too much, or is it all alright? With the children analogy, is 'sensible lad' leading the others in a game of football, in which case you can safely return to whatever you were trying to do, or has 'little horror' shifted their attention towards tormenting the cat or scaling the neighbour's tree, in which case intervention is called for? Tasha could see it that way as she was indeed often left in charge of her younger brothers and their friends when she had her own things to get on with and did not want to have to spend all her time policing them.

In Tasha's case, the 'aspects of self' work was crucial for moving things on. Being able to own 'Good Tasha' meant she had access to the resource of her nan's love for and belief in her. Combined with building a new relationship with the past using anger and self-compassion, this laid a foundation from which it was possible to make progress on the self-harm, and on striking a balance in her thorny relationship with her mother.

Conclusion and summary

Hopefully, this chapter has demonstrated the potential of working with the different aspects of the self to open up new possibilities and clear blocks to make way for untapped potential to be explored. This approach goes along with the strengths bow on the formulation diagram to make CCC a truly forward looking and hopeful therapy. However, this cannot succeed where the wounds laid down deep within the self by past trauma and adversity are not addressed. The chapter, along with other chapters in this section, also illustrated how these can be worked with, using the emotions of anger, to gain: a sense of having had a right to better in the past, and so a right to better in the present; compassion to meet the suffering of the past self and clear away the unfair legacy of blame and shame; and sadness – tears to meet the loss of what should have been.

Raju has been neglected recently, because he was not in a place to make use of this type of in-depth therapy. That could well become relevant further down the line. However, he has not been forgotten, and the next chapter will pursue the CCC approach into the further shores of unshared reality, and the programme to address this that Raju encountered in the mental health unit.

17 Beyond the self, beyond the consensus

Introductory summary

So far, the chapters about the intervention phase of CCC have mainly concentrated on Kath and Tasha, because Raju's situation was different in a number of ways. He was in hospital, under the care of an MDT, so that the therapy was only part of the story. Also, the form his breakdown took was different and psychotic. In other words, it transported him into 'unshared reality'. This chapter picks up ideas introduced in Chapters 8 and 9, and concentrates on ways of helping someone navigate between this 'shared and unshared' reality. This form of breakdown is presented in a non-stigmatizing way that allows for the positives that can come from exploration of these reaches of the mind. This novel perspective is helpful in engaging people and motivating them to take responsibility for their safety, which is necessarily a concern in such cases.

The basis for the CCC understanding of psychosis is still ICS, and is captured in the diagrams, Figure 1.1 and Figure 5.1. Psychosis, anomalous experiencing, unshared reality – whatever you like to call it – becomes accessible when the two central meaning making systems are in desynchrony, and this happens at high and at low arousal. In previous chapters, we have seen how interventions such as mindfulness and engagement in activity in the present are important for helping someone reach wise mind or, in this case, shared reality. In this chapter we will learn more about the programme for managing unshared reality (or psychosis) that Raju attends in the hospital. We will see that this is the first stage, starting him on the road towards a sounder way to come to terms with what has happened to him, and to get him back into communication with both his wife and the MDT.

The chapter concludes by looking more widely at ways that people can be affected by psychosis, and the particular role of the Spiritual Crisis Network in offering an alternative perspective.

The fluid self

The preceding section on working with aspects of self illustrates the way in which 'the self' is not a given but a patchwork, a shifting sands comprised of relationships, moods and experiences, weaving in and out between past, present and future.

DOI: 10.4324/9781003081616-21

Each of us constantly navigates this patchwork of potentials, unaware of the process so long as the goal, a good enough sense of self, is achieved. As discussed in previous chapters, wobbles in this comfortable place can occur easily; a grating interaction with others, a lapse in our own efficiency. Mental health breakdown generally means that the balancing act of maintaining this good enough sense of self has failed and that the precarious balance is lost. Efforts to regain it precipitate further crises, and normal functioning collapses to a greater or lesser degree.

In Raju's case, it can be surmised that the intolerable sense of failure in his career pushed this sensitive individual beyond the threshold, beyond consensual reality. This fits with Mike Jackson's 'problem solving' model of psychosis introduced in Chapter 9 (Jackson 2010). For Raju, temporarily crossing the threshold helped. He found another world where new meaning was revealed to him and where he had an important role. That this was unshared and ungrounded in physical as well as more general consensus reality led to hospitalization and diagnosis. The hospital offered a new identity; that of a mental patient with a putative diagnosis of schizophrenia. The effect on his sense of self can be guessed at, and his first instinct was to reject it angrily.

In Chapter 2, the effect of diagnosis on stigma, meaning a damaged sense of self, was discussed, along with the movements within psychology and psychiatry to counter this. More was said about alternative conceptualizations and research indicating the beneficial effects of such alternatives in Chapter 9. However, on admission to hospital, Raju, along with most other people accessing mental health services in crisis, was offered no alternative. He either accepts their version of his 'self' and complies willingly with treatment, or is stuck in limbo with no obvious way forward.

The Raju dilemma

This also posed a dilemma for the team who had limited beds and needed to stabilize people and discharge them as soon as possible, but with no hint of compliance from Raju, there was no guarantee that he would not discontinue medication and so increase risk in future. The medication had in fact caused him to be less sure about his 'reality', but since he was refusing to talk to anyone senior about his beliefs and experiences, there was no means of knowing that. A further complication concerned where to discharge him to. He was furious with Ambika and his family for their part in committing him, and refusing to speak to them, so it was by no means certain that he could return to his home.

At this stage, it was likely that for Raju, the whole situation felt just too conflicted, with no 'good enough' sense of self in sight. The other world that had previously been his refuge was becoming both less real and less welcoming. Since admission, even before medication, the experiences and messages had started to turn hostile, so offered no welcome escape anymore. However, it can be surmised that when he allowed himself to entertain the alternative, a life sentence as a mental patient, a void of depression and hopelessness opened up from which he instinctively drew back.

So, he settled down to making the best of things in the present. For all of us, our relationships with the other people around us are crucial for getting by, particularly in an unfamiliar and unwelcome situation, and for Raju, the people in his orbit seemed to have become divided between friends and enemies. He was comfortable doing his art work with encouragement from the OT, talking to the nursing assistant who shared his cultural background, attending mindfulness and other groups run by the assistant psychologist, and spending time with a subset of the other patients with whom he had made friends. The senior members of the team such as the psychiatrists, the clinical psychologist and the trained nurses appeared to him to be in league with 'the enemy', and so he avoided them, and communicated with them as little as possible when cornered. He refused to meet Ambika or the family. Sticking with this rather limited circle meant he did not have to face his irresolvable dilemmas.

The 'What is Real' group

We have already seen in Chapter 13 the beginnings of a breach in this stand-off, where the assistant psychologist persuaded Raju to join a group on the ward, run by the clinical psychologist, which offered a different approach, and one with the potential to open up possibilities beyond the stark choice outlined above.

First, a word about this group, which has been developed and delivered within a number of acute mental health services. It delivers the CCC perspective on psychosis, usually in four sessions designed for acute services where stays are short, but a longer version has been used in the community. There is one published evaluation: Owen et al. (2015), a manual (available at: www.isabelcla rke.org/docs/What_is_real_programme.pdf) and an unpublished evaluation (Wilson, Clarke & Philips 2009, retrievable from: www.isabelclarke.org/docs/Stigma_paper_CP&P.doc).

Raju and the group

This group, and conversations with the assistant psychologist about the content in between the four sessions, helped Raju to find new ways of looking at his situation. The whole issue of unusual and unshared experiences, whether hearing or seeing things that others don't, or being convinced where others are distinctly unconvinced, was presented in a wider context of human potential. Group members identified that people take drugs and undertake extreme spiritual practice to achieve the same sort of states, but that the experience is usually more controllable when deliberately chosen in this way. The group considered the pros and cons of shared and unshared reality. The general consensus was that shared reality was boring whereas unshared could be exciting and 'buzzy'. They also recognized that unshared reality led to loneliness and isolation, and had its dangers. After all, it had ultimately landed them all in hospital.

The idea of unshared reality was becoming easier for Raju to accept, as it was explained that anyone could enter this state, so did not imply defectiveness. Almost anyone would access it if subjected to extreme experiences such as extended solitary confinement as in hostage accounts. However, access was easier for some, the 'high Schizotypes', than for others. It was explained that high Schizotypy does not mean that someone is ill, and further, it is associated, as shown by research, with gifts, such as creativity, as well as vulnerability (Claridge 1997). This was an important revelation for Raju. It enabled him to see himself as someone who did have the propensity to trip off into states where others would not follow, but that this went with his identity as a sensitive and creative person, which had been until then quite vigorously squashed. He started to be able to see his breakdown as something of a wake-up call.

This realization meant that the next phase of the programme made a lot of sense. This introduced coping strategies to help people manage their realities, or 'symptoms' to use the medical terminology. He was encouraged to chart when his convictions were stronger or weaker. The participants found that their logging of the danger times agreed, when they compared results of this monitoring. The charts showed that stressful, and drifting times, such as trying to get to sleep or when nothing much was happening, were when unshared reality had a chance to creep in. Keeping active, with the mind focused on the activity, assumed new importance, along with having ordinary, probably 'boring', conversations. A further group programme on the ward, about stress management, was recommended to teach breathing and relaxation skills in order to bring down stress levels, along with tackling life challenges that produce stress.

Mindfulness was introduced in the third session of the group as a way of observing what is going on in the mind from a detached position, where it is possible to decide whether or not to go along with the voices or beliefs; to 'give them power'. Members of the group plagued by critical voices found this could bring relief. They could note the voice without having to believe it or do what it was directing. The fourth session introduced the idea of this type of breakdown as problem solving. Group members could identify that their first episode had occurred at times of stress and transition, when no straight way forward in life presented itself. Unshared reality offered a sideways move, which had the potential to open up new possibilities, but also the danger of getting ensnared in a half-life. Learning to manage the threshold safely was the key to avoiding this outcome.

For Raju, the mindfulness introduced within the group was challenging. He had found mindfulness on the ward quite calming. Often that gave him a break by allowing a short period of focusing on one thing at a time; a particular object or eating a raisin, for instance. Mindfulness as conducted in the What is Real group invited him to consider his convictions as just ideas that had taken residence in his mind, but that he did not need to accept in their entirety. This choice felt disturbing and made him uneasy.

Coming to terms with shared reality

Following the group, the assistant psychologist, who had built a good rapport with Raju, persuaded him to have some sessions with the clinical psychologist. The second session started something like this:

CP: Last time you said that you found the group interesting, particularly hearing what the others had to say. You realized that there were a lot of similarities. But also, the idea that things were not always how they seemed; that there wasn't necessarily a straight answer to 'What is Real', and that mindfulness helped to get to a place where you could see that, was challenging. It takes courage to recognize that things you were really certain of might be more complicated. Have you tried mindfulness on your own? What do you feel about that now?

R: It all keeps shifting anyway, and it was getting really dark, so I can see I have to be careful. I now see that it is dangerous when it gets into things that might kill me. But there was a lot that was good – I am getting some of that into the pictures. I used to draw a long time ago, when I was at school, but these are different. I couldn't have done them before I was shown those things. The group is right that all this helps with art.

CP: Yes, and everyone agrees that your pictures are really exciting – they get across. When you talked about your experiences and what you were being told before, you lost people.

R: I can see now that they just thought it was mad.

CP: And now you know that there are different ways of looking at it. If you let it take over, mad is probably the word for it, but if you can be sure to keep at least one foot firmly in the shared world, you can use your new insights and share them in a way that gets across to people and does not alienate them. How do you feel about that?

R: Disappointing, but also in a way reassuring.

CP: Have you got a sense from the group of what you need to do in order to manage that?

R: Well, the mindfulness is useful. Doing things like talking to people and doing art helps. But I don't think I could have managed any of those things before I came into hospital. I was too out of it. I hate to admit it, but the medication probably has made that possible, though I don't like the way it slows me down and fuddles my thinking.

CP: I am inclined to agree that the medication was helpful in getting you to this point. In the long term you can certainly develop your own skills for managing shared and unshared reality to keep yourself on the right side of it, but for now, medication will make it easier, and if you say that in ward round, the team will look more favourably on discharge.

This turn of events did indeed go down well in ward round, the next day, but brought to a head the problem of where Raju should go on discharge. The next session with the psychologist focused on relations with Ambika and the family.

CP: Can we look at how you feel about Ambika as this does really affect the future. When I met her, I got the sense that she really cared about you and wanted the best for you, but I appreciate that you feel differently.

R: They all turned against me. They brought those people into the house to drag me off into hospital. How can I trust them?

CP: That must have been a horrible experience, and I can see that it felt as if people you had trusted had betrayed you. But there might be another side to it. Could we explore a bit what might have been going on for Ambika? Do you think she might have been worried? After all, you were intending to kill yourself. Can you think back to before all this happened, if you had had cause to fear that Ambika might die, how would you have felt?

R: It would have been awful. I totally loved her. That is why all this is so terrible.

CP: So could we guess that that was how it felt for her, as I do believe she loves you?

R: Yes, I see that. But why did she have to bring those people in and drag me off to hospital?

CP: You tell me. How else could she have kept you safe? It could be that ensuring that you stayed alive was her top priority.

R: OK. Maybe.

CP: It would be better to be able to discuss all this with her – we are just guessing here. I would be happy to see the two of you together if you would agree. What do you think?

The joint meeting enabled Ambika to get off her chest the sickening worry she had been experiencing, and Raju was able to realize that she had only consented to his sectioning when she could see no other way to ensure his safety, and that her constant love for him was behind it.

Ambika also related how much she had been conscious that he had been struggling in the period leading up to the breakdown. She had always been aware of how his family had dominated him; his father had dictated his career and his brothers had bullied and made fun of him. She could see that he hated his job and that it was not right for him. She repeated the suggestion that he should change career to something more suited to his real aptitudes, and that if, as was likely, this entailed a period out of employment while he studied for a new qualification, he could be the main homemaker and carer, assuming they managed to start a family.

This proposition still felt very threatening for Raju and his sense of who he was; his identity. He could just imagine how his family would react; what would they say to the wider circle of relatives, etc.? However, sooner or later they would have to own up to his breakdown to that wider circle, and even a diagnosis of schizophrenia. Ambika gently suggested that maybe it was time to stand up to them all. The psychologist agreed and promised some positive anger work to assist this.

Other manifestations of 'psychosis'

Raju's situation is one example of how straying into unshared reality can affect someone. In diagnostic language, he was suffering from delusions, which had both a grandiose (he felt chosen and important) and a paranoid (there was a conspiracy against him) element to them. There is, of course, a wide variety of other places that unshared reality can take people to.

Hearing voices, or seeing things that others do not is very common, along with other disturbing sensory experiences, such as feeling, smelling and experiencing touch in the absence of any physical stimulus. This can be seen as part of the breaking down of the normal distinction between internal and external events, memory and current reality, as discussed in Chapter 8.

In Chapter 5, the link between trauma and psychosis was discussed. This sort of fragmentation goes naturally with past traumatic events that over-whelm the capacity to make the necessary links between the emotional and rational processing systems in the brain, and hence leave undigested material as a sort of threat system lurking in the implicational. This emerges at times of crisis in the present. For instance, voices often, but not always, reflect threatening relationships in the individual's past. This sort of presentation can be worked with by re-forging a relationship with neglected and unde-veloped aspects of the self, represented by the voice, in a similar manner to working with aspects of self. Voice dialogue is a recognized approach (e.g. Svanholmer & May 2018, Stone & Stone 1993).

Paranoia is a very common unshared experience, and the unrealistic fears involved here can be traced back to real threat, both in the distant past such as childhood, but often more recently as well. Substance abuse is frequently a factor in paranoia, whether as self-medication, or just going along with social group and lifestyle, and for a vulnerable individual this both fuels the paranoia and locks them in a social world fraught with realistic threat (e.g. drug debts).

The place of spirituality

The overlap between spirituality and psychic phenomena, and travelling over the threshold, has been discussed in Chapter 4. Even people who previously had no interest in religion or spirituality find themselves preoccupied by this at such times, as in the case of Raju. The breaking down of boundaries leads to experiencing relationship beyond the limits imposed by the rational mind, i.e. the propositional and implicational working in sync. Experience of relation-ship, including relationship with the divine or spirit entities, is real, even where the object eludes precise, propositional, knowledge and verification. In the same way, dissolution of boundaries opens the way to psychic knowing and communication, which, in our binary world, might be real or, more likely, illusory, but which stands in a realm governed by the logic of both/and where this distinction breaks down.

The way in which this class of experience is dismissed by psychiatry can be particularly hurtful to people who have received revelatory insights, as we can see from Raju's angry reaction. It is also short-sighted, as there is plenty of evidence that these insights, if interpreted broadly and not taken literally, can in fact open the way to transformative experience. Grof and Grof (1991) has already been cited in this context in Chapter 9. I have gathered a number of examples in Clarke (2010a), my book on psychosis and spirituality, for instance in the chapters by Janice Hartley and Caroline Brett (Hartley 2010, Brett 2010).

In the UK, the Spiritual Crisis Network (SCN, www.spiritualcrisisnetwork. uk) offers this perspective and provides individual email contact and local support groups for people for whom this is a more positive light in which to view a breakdown. With the pandemic, it has become necessary to offer these groups over Zoom, and out of this necessity has developed a Zoom support group that can be accessed from anywhere. This has proved an invaluable resource that will continue, should normal life ever resume.

The advice given by SCN is clear on the need for safety; grounding in the present, attending to the physical – food, sleep, etc. and maintaining social contact, as well as involving the mental health services if there is any suggestion of risk. At the same time, SCN takes seriously the spiritual side of the experiences and their potential for positive transformation – if handled in a sensible and grounded manner.

It should be added that the Open Dialogue approach, introduced in Chapter 9, also takes seriously the perspective of the service user, and so is open to hearing spiritual and other non-pathologizing ways of making sense of anomalous experiences.

Conclusion and summary

This chapter brings to a close the fourth section, and with it, the part of the book that provides detailed exposition of how CCC can be applied in clinical practice. This chapter has covered the CCC approach to the sort of mental breakdown that takes the individual away from consensual reality and into stranger realms of experience. The case of Raju has illustrated how this psychotic form of breakdown can be conceptualized in a more humane and less alienating form, in a manner that has a chance of salvaging something of the individual's sense of self.

The whole book has emphasized both the importance and the fragility of this sense of self. Taking the blunt instrument of a devastating diagnosis to it, without corrective information, is likely to be as destructive to mental health going forward as the original breakdown, as the research quoted in Chapter 9 suggests. In Raju's case, which is based on clinical experience of working in a particular mental health unit (see Clarke & Wilson 2008, Durrant et al. 2007) over a period of eight years, providing this wider context enabled him to come to terms with his situation. This made it possible for him to start to mend relations with both his wife and the MDT. In this way, he was left in a situation where his safety (and Ambika's) was being monitored and supported, and the seeds of a new direction for his life had been sown.

The wider spectrum of psychotic presentations was then reviewed, along with the role of alternative responses. The Spiritual Crisis Network and Open Dialogue are the two examples given.

The next chapter will conclude the story for our three example cases, and consider the wider way in which a CCC therapy might operate, not concentrated purely within the individual, but reaching out and engaging wider sources of support, and providing direction for this support across a lifetime. This is in line with the philosophy of seeing the individual as making sense embedded within their circles of roles and relationships.

Section V

Wrapping up and wider horizons

This section will consider 'where next' for our three case examples, who have all been left, deliberately, in a relatively unresolved state. This will give a sense of the place of a CCC therapy in someone's life journey; not a tidy solution, but a creative stage along the way. The section will then cover the place of CCC in the wider spectrum of the mental health services, citing research and evaluation both published and current, along with some of the trials of getting new ideas accepted. The book concludes with some yet wider speculations.

DOI: 10.4324/9781003081616-22

Section V

Wrapping up and wider horizons

18 The end is the beginning
Therapy as toolkit

Introductory summary

This chapter will give a rounding off account of the therapies for Kath, Tasha and Raju, with a sense of where that leaves them in the life-long journey of finding out and creating who they are and will become. This process might or might not include more formal therapy, but it will surely involve the roles and relationships, the whole social context, that is an integral part of their being. This leads on to discussion of 'the toolbox'; the idea of the therapy as providing a set of skills and pointers that should be kept accessible and referred to throughout life.

Crucial for the aim of this book, which is to help the helpers, this toolbox should be shared knowledge, because the more support to manage in the way directed by the formulation and goals the individual can muster, the better. For close supporters, the formulation can also be shared, as it demonstrates where the effort needs to be directed. How much is revealed of this essentially personal document is of course at the discretion of the individual. Where someone is under the care of a team, or a number of professionals (for instance, Tasha was under the CMHT, had an individual therapist, and was being supported by her tutor at college), it is helpful if the formulation can be shared across the board, so that everyone is supporting the person in the same way and to the same end.

The chapter concludes by giving due weight to the external, societal factors that impinged upon all our three examples, and helped to produce the intolerable internal felt sense that the therapy was addressing. This is to acknowledge the severe limitations of what can be achieved by therapy, as it acts upon internal space, and so much of relevance is out there, in the environment. This is especially true in the current context of deteriorating public services and increasing inequality, factors that inevitably bear most heavily on those vulnerable to mental breakdown.

How long is a piece of string?

Our three therapy cases have been left, at the end of the previous section, at some random point in the middle of the intervention, skills development, phase of their therapies. The ideal length for a psychological therapy is subject

DOI: 10.4324/9781003081616-23

for debate. There is research on this, which is brought together by the UK NICE guidelines, which make recommendations for length of treatment that has been found to be effective across different presentations (expressed in the medical terms of diagnosis and symptom reduction). For instance, the Borderline Personality Disorder (Tasha's diagnosis) guidelines recommend that brief therapy of less than three months' duration is not suitable for this presentation (National Institute for Health and Clinical Excellence 2009, 1.3.4.4).

CCC approaches this issue differently. More will be said about the application and history of CCC in Chapter 19, but for now it is relevant to know that its principal development took place within Acute Mental Health services, where people are admitted and discharged with bewildering rapidity. Even in these conditions, we were able to demonstrate some effect with a vanishingly brief, formulation based, intervention, backed up by relevant group work (Araci & Clarke 2017, Durrant et al. 2007). More recently, this result has been backed up by research conducted in the Acute Inpatient Service of the South London and Maudsley Trust, who found benefit from a one-session CCC formulation intervention (Bullock et al. 2020).

Adapting the approach for the primary care, IAPT, service, the number of linked individual and group sessions is 17 or 18. However, the length of time over which these are delivered can vary, as there is often, but not always, a gap, sometimes of months, between the individual sessions and the group. It is argued that this is acceptable within the model, as, once someone has the formulation, which they have helped to work out and which enables them to see clearly what they need to do in order to break the vicious cycles and move forward, they can take responsibility for that process. Some people find that the initial four formulation sessions are sufficient.

Kath and Tasha received an individual form of CCC, where there is scope to adapt the number of sessions to the needs of that person. The concept of handing over responsibility to make the changes to the individual is the same here as for the linked individual and group programme. Post formulation, the focus is on behaviour change, on achieving the identified goals, and the therapy provides support and guidance with this. Ultimately, it is down to the individual to effect change.

The group programme (available in Clarke & Nicholls 2018) covers a variety of emotionally and existentially challenging topics in a short space of time. Furthermore, it is aimed at the people with the most intractable problems within the range of referrals to the service. The facilitators repeat the mantra that the programme can only provide a toolkit. Once the individual has grasped the origins of the problem and what needs to be done through the formulation, they can choose the tools that best suit their predicament, and use them at their own speed to do the work. The group provides support for now, but the work will need to continue, hopefully with further support from those around in the natural environment. All this is no different for the individual form of the therapy.

Inviting natural supporters into sessions fits naturally with this approach, and we have seen how Tasha's mother and Raju's wife have been included. It is important that significant others understand what the individual is working on, so that they can provide relevant support and avoid obstruction. As in the examples of both Tasha's mother and Ambika, those individuals might need space to air what they have been going through emotionally, and have this validated, before they can be available to offer this support. In the case of Tasha, there was a formulation and goals that could be shared, and it is important that CCC formulations are written in such a way that their subject is willing for them to be seen by others. The wording needs to be negotiated to ensure that this is acceptable. All this is very different from some traditional, dependency forming, therapies of indeterminate length (think Woody Allen). DBT pioneered the idea of teaching new ways of coping and providing support to implement them that takes account of the wider system, but DBT approaches it differently.

Concluding the therapies: Kath

In Kath's case, 16 sessions were contracted, as that is seen as a reasonable length of therapy in cases of somewhat intractable depression within the primary care service. This could have been extended, had particular issues arisen that could have been reasonably tackled in three or four further sessions. As it happened, Kath took the message on board, and started to make significant changes, accompanied by decreases in the scores measuring levels of anxiety and depression and effect on life functioning, which were administered each session, as is the practice in IAPT services. She saw the point of mindfulness, and practiced it regularly, applying it in different situations. She had started to be more assertive with family, and more diplomatic at work. This helped her to reduce some sources of stress. The involvement of the police led to the stalker steering clear of her, and though she could not achieve the care she would have wanted for her mother, she did put her foot down about accepting some domiciliary input, which improved that situation. Her mother's deterioration and her dependence on her father remained a source of worry, but she accepted that she had done all she could.

She had managed to keep up attendance at work, even on off days, thus removing the threat to her continued employment. Significantly, she had taken seriously the need to treat herself as she would a good friend. She no longer saw her role merely in terms of being there for others. She gave herself permission to pursue her interest in nature photography, and joined a course, engaging a babysitter for about the first time ever. She also got involved in local nature conservancy work, along with her daughter who shared this passion, and started to meet people. Life was just beginning to open up a little.

The therapist took care to bring up the subject of the approaching ending in each of the last four sessions. He encouraged Kath to express her anxiety about this, and tried hard to elicit the natural anger that goes with a sense of abandonment. This was important, as they had formed a strong bond, and there is always a danger of a serious dip in mood following the end of the therapy when that support is withdrawn and the individual feels bereft. It is vital to allow expression of those feelings within the therapy.

The therapist also cautioned Kath against seeing the inevitable return of the depression as a disaster to be feared, but rather as a temporary dip. He advised she could manage this by treating herself with kindness and understanding, along with not allowing everything to slip – the balancing act. There is a danger arising from the medical perspective where ups and downs of mood are viewed as something that must be fixed then and there, and the immediate effectiveness of anti-depressants when someone presents for the first time reinforces this. Unfortunately, in cases of recurrent depression like Kath's, diminishing returns set in, and after a while there is no new miracle, only unpleasant withdrawal effects when the person decides they want to free themselves from the dependency.

Kath was seen for the last time by the therapist after three months for a follow-up appointment. She was maintaining her gains. She had been through some bumpy periods in the meantime, but had kept up her wider circle of activity and was becoming more socially active. One year later, she again contacted the service. Her mother had died, and she found the past sweeping over her again, along with a degree of anger towards her father that she had not thought herself capable of. The therapist was still with the service and offered her four booster sessions, to talk about how she felt and rehearse the skills to help her manage. This reminder put her back on track, along with the prospect of targeted bereavement counselling through a local charity.

Tasha

Tasha's therapy did not end as tidily as Kath's. When an agreement was reached to conclude therapy at 24 sessions, extended over about six months, she had made some major gains. The self-harm had all but stopped, and Tasha had acquired skills to manage it, using mindfulness to divert her attention onto something else when she felt the urge. Video games on her phone came in handy here. She made a significant gain in the softening of the fierce self-hatred that had impeded progress earlier in the therapy. She gained an appreciation of herself and her potential, which offered hope of a possible future where she could make use of her intelligence and talents to pursue a real career.

However, she put off the access course for a year, having left it too late to apply (deliberately?). Her mother's ambivalence and her entanglement in that relationship remained a problem. She was just too useful at home as a carer for her brothers and a source of cash.

Intimate relationships were identified as a problem area in the course of therapy. Tasha became more aware that she was letting herself down by going for brief sexual encounters with essentially undesirable types, thus leaving herself open to abuse. She could now see that a more satisfactory sort of relationship was possible. She came closer to entertaining the 'boring' but decent lad who was interested in her, but tended to treat him abominably, so it was at best on-off.

In the course of the therapy, she did, however, become aware of what was behind this unhelpful pattern of relating. Close relationships had been so utterly painful in the past that behind the bravado of going for the buzz and talk of the other boy being boring was raw, visceral fear of becoming vulnerable to someone who could hurt her that much again, and awareness that real sexual intimacy would entail that vulnerability. However, having managed to engage once in therapy, there was every chance that this could be tackled in a future therapy when the time was right.

The same went for the issue of the sexual abuse, which, though named and identified as significant in the formulation, had never become a major focus of the therapy. It was still there in the background, distorting her sense of who she was and as another factor in her dysfunctional relationship to sex. However, its immediacy that had helped fuel the self-harm was diminished, and it had been disentangled from her feelings towards her nan, so that tackling it through a future therapy, perhaps one entailing re-living, would be more possible.

On the relationship with her nan, Tasha had made real progress. She had glimpsed that she could be someone her nan would be proud of. She had the potential. She could start to understand why she had gone off the rails, to forgive her child self, and distance herself from the judgements of the abuser – and of her mother. This was a basis for hope for the future, and this aspect seemed to have consolidated at follow up, though Tasha and her therapist agreed that there was still work to be done, when she was ready.

As with Kath, the discussion of the impending ending took place in each of the last six sessions. However, Tasha had found the therapy emotionally challenging, and part of her was quite relieved to contemplate the ending. In some ways, the biggest achievement of this therapy had been engagement, and orienting Tasha to the notion that she could, with support, make changes to her situation.

Raju

Engagement was even more central for what was achieved in Raju's case. He only managed a couple of sessions with the clinical psychologist, plus the joint session with Ambika, before discharge from the Acute Mental Health Service. During the admission, most of the work had been achieved outside of formal therapy and through the various groups and in interaction with other members of the team, and indeed, fellow patients. There had been no individual formulation. It would be perfectly possible to construct one, and the CP had one at the back of her mind. However, for someone feeling as open to outside influence and vulnerable as Raju, to formulate collaboratively could have been experienced as intrusive and dangerous. The States of Mind diagram explaining shared and unshared reality (Figure 8.1) was enough.

It was important for the success of this approach that a significant part of the inpatient therapeutic programme was linked to the CCC model. This is the case in a number of areas of the UK that have adopted the approach (more on this in the next chapter). Not everyone in the team was on board, as we have seen in the case of one of the psychiatrists, but with a comprehensive group programme and enough staff at different levels within the team to back it up, this was an issue to be worked around. Indeed, it was the programme that ultimately persuaded Raju to work with the system and accept medication (for now).

On discharge from hospital, Raju remained under the Home Treatment Team, the community arm of the Acute Mental Health Service, in order to provide fairly intensive monitoring, and during this period, he was allowed to return to the unit to complete the group programmes he had started as an inpatient, which included an Emotional Coping Skills Group. This covered the ways of managing emotions positively discussed in earlier chapters, and was particularly important for him in regard to owning and making positive use of his anger.

On discharge from the Acute Service, the Early Intervention in Psychosis service took him on and offered support and therapy – CBT for psychosis – for a couple of years. During this period, he put a lot of energy into his art to start with, but as the intense experiences of his breakdown faded, he turned his attention to pure mathematics, and was able to enrol on a Master's course, and so start to pursue the career he had wanted following university. As he needed clear thinking to do this, he gradually, and with medical supervision, came off his medication.

An important part of his journey back was finding communities on the internet that recognized the positive potential of high Schizotypy and anomalous experiencing, such as the Spiritual Crisis Network UK. Ambika joined him in this interest, as she had supported him in all his moves to change career direction, and to stand up to his family's opposition. Through these alternative forums, Raju was able to meet people who had gone through what he experienced and worse, but had emerged to live more fulfilled lives than before, sometimes training as mental health professionals in order to be able to help others, using the insight gained by their own journey. These contacts enabled him to build on the beginnings of a positive identity as a traveller in the transliminal; a journey started in the hospital; at the same time as taking responsibility for keeping his feet on the ground, and managing threatened relapses when stress levels increased. Ambika's support was vital here.

No cure for life

So, none of our three illustrative case studies ended up 'cured'. It would be truer to say that they were all set off on a journey, equipped with their toolkit of skills. Mindfulness is the central skill in the toolkit, as it makes possible the breaking of the habitual pattern of behaviour and the substitution of something different. This is hard, and the terrible emotions that drove those habitual patterns do not go away overnight. They need to be worn down slowly, and overlaid with the positive experiences that come from approaching things differently.

The assumption, implicit in the way much therapy research is framed, that therapy is an intervention that can be viewed as parallel to medication leads to an expectation that 'cure' is the desired outcome. CCC rejects this assumption. There is no cure for life. At the end of their episodes of therapy, Kath, Tasha and Raju had in common that they were set on a road that pointed to a more satisfactory version of themselves; one that was more liveable and with more potential than the intolerable internal felt sense that had driven them into therapy in the first place. This would not solve all their problems. However, the point they had each reached at the end held out the hope of a more secure place to face the situations that life was bound to throw at them in the future (they had yet to encounter COVID-19, for instance).

The inevitability of these future challenges links to another feature of all these three cases; their mental health issues were not just about internal events. External circumstances and pressures played a huge part for each one. Some of those circumstances were current. Kath's mother's situation coincided with her being pursued by her ex. Her difficulties at work were in turn partly a product of the impact of those stresses on her performance.

In Tasha's case, the most important adverse external circumstances took place years earlier; being removed from her nan's; abuse and neglect leading to behaviour that made her ashamed. Because of the way the threat system in the implicational confuses past and present, these were as raw as if they were current, and mixed with the difficult circumstances of her current life, such as the sharply conflicted relationship with both her disabled brother and her mother, it was not surprising that she stumbled from one unsatisfactory way of managing her internal state to another. For Raju as well, past and present combined to such an intolerable degree that his ability to escape into another dimension offered the only way out.

The therapy profession, along with psychiatry, has long been criticized for locating the problem within the individual and so masking the ills of society (Pilgrim 2015), and there is currently a major movement within psychology to both acknowledge the social dimension behind mental health issues and to develop a 'social cure' (Haslam et al. 2018). The Power Threat Meaning Framework initiative (Division of Clinical Psychology 2018) covered in Chapter 2, stresses power imbalance and the role of destructively exercised power in mental health presentations. There is plenty of evidence for an association between societal factors such as poverty, migration, racism, etc. and mental health challenge. Other societal ills, such as child abuse and domestic violence, are heavily implicated, and are often but not invariably linked to poverty and social deprivation.

Our three cases illustrate some but not all these circumstances. Kath's call centre job falls into the category of employment often linked to exploitation, and she was twice a victim of domestic violence. The problem of securing adequate care for her elderly mother was exacerbated by her father's attitude, but even if this had been more reasonable, affordable, good quality dementia care provision is not something our society has prioritized. Raju suffered from racial bullying along with the pressures from his family. Tasha's short life was beset by multiple disadvantages in terms of abuse, neglect, questionable judicial decision (why was she returned to her mother's care?), as well as suffering the effects on the household of inadequate provision for her severely disabled brother, all in the context of falling within a low socio-economic band, with associated low expectations.

All these pressures point to the effect of growing societal inequality and the sorts of political priorities that have dominated in recent times. Identifying the political and social dimension to mental health challenges does not mean that therapy has no role. Therapy simply needs the humility to know its place. All three case studies illustrate the potential for empowerment, along with 'wise mind' management of adverse circumstances that cannot be immediately altered. The CCC formulation aims to identify all factors in the situation, both external and internal, and to clarify which are within the individual's control for intervention. Both feeling helpless and unrealistic expectations are paralyzing. CCC acknowledges the outside forces, both past and present, behind the individual's predicament and normalizes breakdown, both in the context of those forces, and the factors common to all human beings that ICS brings to the fore: the intrusion of past threat into present coping and the lack of a 'boss'. Mindful exercise of balance and tolerance of uncertainty lies at the heart of the approach, and the weight of societal challenges tries this exercise of balance to the limit.

Conclusion and summary

This chapter has concluded the 'story' of our three composite case examples, and sent them on their way. They were designed to illustrate a representative range of the main mental health challenges. Of course, they only cover this range to an extent, and many possible presentations are left out. There is no hint of Obsessive Compulsive Disorder (OCD), eating disorders or addictions within these examples. Hopefully, the way that CCC considers any mental health challenge, as a way of managing an intolerable internal state, that is intolerable for a discoverable reason, in a manner that works short term but keeps the individual trapped, can be applied by the reader to these, or any other, diagnoses. I have always found this possible within extensive clinical practice.

These cases have illustrated how this approach can help orientate someone to take charge for themselves of the way forward, even in challenging circumstances, and provides the tools to do this. The chapter then turned to the issue of those challenging circumstances, as this was the context for each of the three breakdowns illustrated here. This reinforces the point that environmental pressures and deficiencies need to be given due weight when seeking to understand breakdown. Equally, environmental solutions are key. Raju needed to find a new direction in life. Kath was helped by engaging with nature.

The next chapter will turn attention to the development and spread of the CCC model itself, and sketch in how it came about and where and how it is being applied, along with future directions. It will also address the thorny issue of gaining recognition by inclusion in the evidence base, necessary for a new approach, however widely it might have proved its worth and gained acceptance on the ground.

19 CCC in the wider world

Introductory summary

This chapter traces the history and dissemination of the CCC approach. As this name is comparatively recent, and it has been previously known under other acronyms and labels (ISP, EFFA, the Woodhaven Approach), its origins and the length of time it has been around have remained largely invisible. The approach has been developed in response to clinical challenges; an outpatient psychological therapies department with an unmanageable waiting list; how to get an acute hospital to deliver holistic care; what to do with the people accessing a primary care IAPT service who do not respond to the prescribed therapies; and providing an acceptable intervention for ethnically diverse populations. These are all areas where strict, diagnostically adherent protocols laid down by an evidence base drawing on large scale, controlled studies, tend to falter. CCC, with its flexibility of delivery and freedom from diagnostic constraints, has provided a practical and acceptable solution in all these instances.

However, proving this according to the criteria required for inclusion in the evidence base has been more challenging, as related in the latter part of this chapter. The chapter ends with consideration of the applicability of CCC to other client groups; forensic, young people and learning disabilities.

Origins

In varied forms and settings, CCC has been around since the late 1990s. It has spread because it has proved useful to services on the ground, and helpful and acceptable to service users. Proving this to the wider world, and gaining the visibility I would suggest it merits, has been held up by a number of factors that will be outlined in this chapter, along with the history of its development. One thing that has certainly impeded recognition is a number of changes of name. When first developed, as a way of both bringing more emotional and relational elements into CBT, and managing referrals in a busy outpatient psychotherapy department without creating a waiting list, it didn't have a name. It was how I enabled the majority of people on my (otherwise unmanageable) assessment list to go off and do the work on their own.

DOI: 10.4324/9781003081616-24

I was able to offer them two or three assessment sessions, in which we completed the CCC formulation (not quite as developed; the strengths bow came later). At that point, the individual was in charge of the process. If they felt they could manage, they were discharged, or they could opt for review and could name the interval for this. With the help of a trainee, I could cope with offering ongoing therapy to the minority for whom this was not going to be enough. With a basis in mindfulness and emphasis on behaviour change, the approach fitted with the developing third wave paradigm, and my training in DBT in 2000 added both the idea of separating off skills training, and many of the techniques for managing emotions.

Woodhaven

In 2004, I became psychological therapies lead for a new-build mental health hospital, and the combination of the simple, emotion-focused formulation, with skills teaching perfectly fitted the task of embedding psychological thinking and psychological approaches into the, traditionally very medical, world of the psychiatric hospital. This was not achieved overnight, but by 2007, along with my colleague Hannah Wilson and our brilliant assistant psychologist, we were able to publish a modest evaluation (Durrant et al. 2007), and the next year, an edited book (Clarke & Wilson 2008). This book was not exclusively about the way of working pursued in Woodhaven, our hospital, but half the chapters were written either by ourselves or members of our team. Chapters were contributed by the OT, a nurse and a mental health practitioner, reflecting the way that CCC enabled a whole team to become involved with delivering therapy.

The formulations were arrived at, collaboratively with the service user, by the psychologists or staff working under their close supervision, and increasingly the whole team was trained and involved in the approach. The groups that comprised the intervention – mindfulness, arousal management, self-compassion and psychotic symptom management (What is Real) – were increasingly run by nurses. The important Emotional Coping Skills Group programme was well supported by DBT training available throughout the Trust. The formulation also informed the thinking of the entire team, even where engagement of the individual was not possible, through regular Case Discussion Meetings (Clarke 2015). These were specifically requested by the nursing team in addition to psychology led reflective practice meetings, which are a staple of clinical psychologist input to team working.

This approach, working at its best, is illustrated in the composite case of Raju. Anyone familiar with acute services will be aware that there are immense challenges, and Woodhaven was no exception. At best, we had a multi-disciplinary team, proud to be involved in an innovative initiative, putting a holistic, psychological approach at the heart of their work. This was dependent on sufficient staffing levels, support from management, skill mix including enough therapy, etc. and there were lean times. The End Word of the 2008 book offers the 'sandcastle' model to those seeking to make acute services more psychological. With the right support, staffing levels and enthusiasm there can be a good period; your sandcastle takes shape. Then, inevitably, the tide comes in. There are incidents that make everyone risk averse, staffing levels dip, management goes off on another tack, and the psychological impetus falters.

At this juncture it is vital not to become discouraged and give up. Wait for the tide to recede and then start building. This is what we did in Woodhaven between 2004 and 2012. As well as a fantastic team dedicated to the work, we had people visiting from all over, and we were invited to deliver training across the country, seeding the same approach in other acute services. There was nothing else out there for acute services with such an ambitious aim. The tide came and went, but then, in 2012, the tsunami hit.

Wider dissemination of the model

Setting these developments in the wider context, the Woodhaven initiative had got off the ground during the good years before the 2008 crash. Following that event, austerity had been eating away at the NHS during the years leading up to 2012, and the Trust was now in financial trouble. Additionally, comparative figures suggested that they had more inpatient beds than other areas. The solution to the financial crisis adopted was therefore to cut beds by one third, meaning the closure of two of the six hospitals in the Trust, and, because of its geographical position, ours was one.

This was a devastating blow to a team with fantastic morale. Many of the nurses used the therapy skills they had acquired to transfer to the IAPT service that was growing at the time. The rest of us moved to another hospital, along with the management. I took retirement, but was charged with a project to embed the (later to be called) CCC approach in the four remaining acute services across the Trust. Along with an assistant psychologist, this was my task 2012–2014, and the results are published in Araci & Clarke (2017). At this stage, the approach was named 'Intensive Support Programme' (ISP).

Meanwhile, CCC training had been delivered quite widely, and the acute services in certain areas had taken it on in a serious manner. Sheffield, Edinburgh, Surrey & Borders and the Northern Health and Social Care Trust in Northern Ireland were early adopters. Paterson et al. (2018) reports on the Edinburgh service, and Bullock et al. (2020), on a recent trial by South London and Maudsley (SLAM). There is more detail on these initiatives in Chapter 14 of Clarke & Nicholls (2018).

The challenge of the evidence base

There are good reasons why CCC has been widely adopted by services. It is intuitively graspable and makes sense. The individual is placed at the heart of the process because the formulation is collaboratively arrived at and agreed. The formulation then gives clear, behavioural, direction. In acute services, and other teams, this provides the goals that can give purpose to the episode of care.

It is, further, in line with the philosophy of the Recovery Approach (Shepherd, Boardman & Slade 2012). 'Recovery' is about listening to the service user, taking their priorities seriously and supporting them to take charge. This tends to take the form of a collaboratively worked out relapse prevention plan (e.g. Wellness Recovery Action Plan, WRAP, Copeland 1997), completed around discharge time. CCC argues that that is too late. The Recovery message needs to be conveyed from the outset, and the individual needs to be acknowledged as central to their care. The role of the team and the service is to provide support to enable the individual to acquire the necessary skills to get their life back on track until they are strong enough to continue using the new coping strategies, helped by their family or system, in the community.

CCC provides a framework to make this happen, with the whole staff team involved in delivering the intervention, whether through groups, or individual coaching and encouragement. Once teams have got their mind around an adjustment in their role, this is normally welcome as offering involvement in the real work of supporting change, as opposed to keeping people safe and waiting for medication to take effect. Managers like it as well, and as it promotes clear goals for admission it can lead to faster throughput, and direction for community support; important in times of bed closures.

Despite all these advantages, there are obstacles to the wider adoption of CCC, and these are to do with the problem of getting the approach into 'the evidence base'. The emphasis on 'evidence-based practice' has gathered momentum over the time of my association with the NHS (as volunteer member of a Community Health Council in the 1980s, and a practitioner from the 1990s). Over this time, I observed various attempts to get control of the juggernaut that is the NHS. General Management, introduced in the 1980s, was only partly successful, and then in 1999, the National Institute for Clinical Excellence (NICE) was founded to ensure that interventions used were those with the strongest scientific basis. (In 2013 it became the National Institute for Health and Care Excellence, but remained NICE.)

This made sense in terms of ensuring effectiveness and, important in the field of therapy, efficient management of a scarce resource. The downside is that the gold standard evaluation of therapies follows the randomized controlled trial (RCT) model used for testing the efficacy of medication. This involves comparison between the intervention to be evaluated and a 'placebo', in such a way that participants have no idea whether they are in the active or the dummy condition. However, finding a convincing 'placebo' for a therapy is a lot harder than for a pill, and randomization in a pressured clinical setting such as an acute psychiatric hospital presents enormous challenges. As mentioned in Chapter 3, NICE is organized around diagnosis, so that the more indeterminate presentations get weeded out. All this removes the gold standard research, which determines what interventions are recommended, further and further away from the complexities and requirements of normal clinical practice. Also, an RCT with the large number of participants needed to look statistically impressive is enormously expensive, so can only be launched by big institutions with established research departments who can successfully bid for major grants.

Aware that published evaluation was the only route to credibility for a new intervention, I have tried. In the 2000s it was still possible to get a small study, conducted with no extra resource, published in a good journal, and that is how Durrant et al. (2007) got out – a paper that has been widely influential. Following that, I tried to interest the Trust's research department in a bigger, funded, study, but this foundered on the impossibility of constructing a control group in an acute setting.

When CCC was rolled out in all four acute services across Hampshire, evaluation and publication was obviously vital, and we conducted three studies, again with no extra resources. The first was an evaluation and feasibility study with the data from over 100 participants quoted, along with details of the groups run and staff involved. This was eventually published after being turned down by a couple of journals (Araci & Clarke 2017). We investigated the impact of the intervention through two qualitative studies using Expert by Experience (EBE) interviewers, one asking staff for their views and the other interviewing service users. The staff study was completed, but has been sent back a couple of times for changes by the journal, and we have not had the resources to push on with it; the second was held up so long by the Ethics Committee that it has not emerged. This rather sorry tale simply illustrates how research publication has become impractical for clinicians on the ground over the last 15 or so years, and is now the preserve of research departments. Even published, Araci & Clarke has had far less impact than Durrant et al. back in 2007, despite being a much larger and more significant study.

The people who don't fit into the boxes

Just as the project to introduce CCC into the Trust's acute services was coming to an end, because the model had been sustainably embedded, in 2014, I was approached by the head of the local IAPT service, Hazel Nicholls. Her service had been funded to explore solutions for the proportion of people (under half) who did not benefit from the NICE recommended therapies – which are mostly straight CBT. The following characteristics for this group had been identified:

- Elements of complex trauma.
- Long therapy history with little evidence of benefit gained.
- Emotion management problems, particularly emotional avoidance.
- Diagnostic complexity.
- Relationship/attachment issues.

Hazel and I adapted CCC for the Hampshire IAPT service (italk) in the form of four individual sessions followed by a 12-week group, with one or two individual review appointments to help people apply the skills learnt in the group to their individual situation. The manual for the programme can be found in Clarke & Nicholls (2018).

This programme has been running for five years and has proved really useful within the service for 'the people who don't fit into the boxes' – a descriptor that appeals to individuals when we are explaining the approach. Clearly, as an innovation within a service dedicated to evidence-based practice and NICE adherent therapies, it needs evaluation, but with absolutely no resource, and an exceptionally stretched service, this was proving elusive.

The culture free project

Help came from an unexpected quarter. I had been slowly working over the internet with a colleague originally from, and with strong links in, Pakistan, but based in Canada, on a CCC manual, designed for diverse ethnicities. Farooq Naeem is one of a team who have been developing culturally adapted forms of CBT (e.g. Naeem et al. 2015, 2016) and wanted to take the project forward with an approach using mindfulness. The features of CCC that make it suitable for cultural adaptation are:

- It follows the individual's experience in an intuitively accessible way with a minimum of theoretical apparatus. It side-steps Western medical conceptualizations of mental distress and the more complex theoretical underpinnings of therapeutic modalities such as conventional CBT and psychodynamic therapies.
- The emphasis on identifying and using only language and descriptors that are natural and comfortable for the individual in the formulation helps to ensure that alien concepts are not being imposed through the use of psychological jargon.
- It uses mindfulness in a targeted and practical manner that does not require extensive practice or commitment to the wider mindfulness tradition, which may not be familiar or acceptable to the individual.
- It lends itself to the involvement of the wider family/social group. The straightforward formulation is easily communicated to important others who can then be recruited as supporters of change for the individual in therapy. The split between the formulation stage and application of new coping skills to the work of breaking the vicious circles identified in the formulation, creates the opportunity for the recruitment of available helpers, as we have seen in the case of mental health teams. In this instance, it can be utilized by natural supporters who will be readily available and will have an interest in helping their relative to recover.
- The ICS theory that underpins CCC paves the way for a model of the human being that embraces both individual self-consciousness, and our embeddedness in the whole. Relationship is accorded a new, more central role. This enables a collectivist view, more in sympathy with many other cultures than our Western, individualistic focus.
- CCC incorporates the individual's strengths and the role of wider, spiritual, connectivity in the task of finding solutions to immediate problems.

Existing therapies have been criticized for being too pathologizing, too individualistic and excluding of religion and spirituality, to suit many other cultures.

This initiative eventually connected me with the Trust's Research and Development Department (R&D) with links to Southampton University. The R&D department funded a small project to test the manual, but struggled to recruit participants, despite Hampshire's ethnically diverse population, until they were able to come to an accommodation with the local IAPT service (italk), on the basis of a reciprocal project to evaluate CCC within italk.

We are still struggling when it comes to publication and we are at the preliminary, small scale pilot project stage with minimal or no funding for both projects. Meanwhile, both have been presented at conferences such as the annual BABCP conferences and the data looks promising. The process of developing the manual for the Culture Free Study, through meeting therapeutic challenges in supervision, has thrown up some fascinating issues. Particularly where religious and spiritual factors complicate the therapy, CCC is well placed to indicate ways forward. Such factors are not of course unique to ethnically diverse populations, and a CCC formulation will always ask about faith or spiritual connection, but it is recognized that this area is more salient for this group, and that has been our experience through the study.

For instance, faith is understood within CCC as experience of relationship, and this offers a way through the following therapeutic dilemma. Westerners (and hence Western therapists), with their strong scientific enculturation, can confuse faith with logic, and so feel helpless faced with a discourse which does not make logical sense to them, while being aware that they should not argue with it. Viewing faith through the lens of logic leads to its being dismissed as misguided, or just 'imagination' (Gilbert 2009 P.213). This perspective misses the lived experience of faith – faith as experience of relationship. One can argue with logical propositions, but not with experience. Bearing this in mind, it is possible to engage with issues of faith without sharing the same faith, provided that faith is recognized as an expression of experienced relationship, because the therapist will know what it feels like to be in relationship. This perspective recognizes that the impulse to worship, obey commandments, etc. is an expression of relationship.

While the object of the relationship (the particular deity, etc.) is fixed, the quality of the relationship is changeable and can be open to discussion. This is where the therapist, treading delicately, can enter into dialogue without detailed knowledge of the particular practice or any experience of faith themselves. For instance, the three Abrahamic faiths (Christianity, Islam and Judaism) share belief in the merciful and compassionate nature of God, which can be a useful corrective to balance fear of judgement. Where the reality of the overall relationship and its centrality is acknowledged, it becomes easier to question specifics, as they need not be essential to the relationship. The implications of faith where they affect the individual's functioning are the legitimate business of the therapist.

This is just one example from a piece of work in progress, which is beyond the scope of this volume, but it does give a sense of this scope and potential of CCC as it is developed.

Potential for other client groups

This book has illustrated the application of CCC to adults of working age with identified mental health difficulties, as these are the main settings where it has been embedded. However, recently, the Older People's Mental Health Services both in my Trust, and another Trust, have received training and are applying the model with good reports and one completed evaluation study being prepared for submission. Training was delivered for our Regional Secure Unit some time ago, where it has been adopted and a research project is planned.

There is interest from adolescent services both here and elsewhere (along with other plans, on hold because of the COVID-19 lockdown). The simplicity and immediacy of the model, and scope for replacing words with pictures, make it appealing both to services for younger people and those with learning disabilities. Where training has been delivered to a mixed group of therapy professionals, practitioners from these services have commented on its applicability. The natural inclusion of helpers and supporters also makes it particularly suitable for these populations. The very basic and immediate way in which mindfulness is introduced and employed is universally graspable, and the ability to come into the present, let go of the emotional pull, and take charge, is not difficult to convey, even where it might be hard to employ in the heat of the moment. Essentially it is a way of making sense of how human beings get stuck, how easy it is for human beings to get stuck and how they might get unstuck – whoever, wherever and whatever age they are!

Conclusion and summary

This chapter has traced the history of CCC through its various applications and name changes. As this history shows, the approach was extensively piloted within one Trust, in response to specific clinical challenges. This led to publications, and interest from elsewhere in the country. CCC became more widely known and recognized through symposia and presentations at conferences, and training workshops were commissioned from diverse places. It came at a time when there was recognition that acute services in particular needed to become more person centred and holistic. The approach was seen as particularly relevant where psychological therapies services were being encouraged to work more closely with teams, in order to ensure wider dissemination of therapeutic approaches. CCC offered a structured way to achieve this that retained specialist expertise at the formulation stage while distributing the intervention more evenly throughout the team. Anyone interested in pursuing this should look at: www.isabelclarke.org/clinical/CBTacute.shtml.

However, in order to gain more general recognition, CCC requires rigorous evaluation, and the trials and tribulations of trying to secure this have been documented, along with cautious hope that we might be starting to get somewhere, with the publication of the SLAM paper (Bullock et al. 2020) and the involvement of the Trust's R&D department. The chapter concluded with a short review of the potential of CCC in a wider array of client groups.

This chapter concludes the substance of the book for those specifically interested in gaining an understanding of mental breakdown, along with practical ways to help and support the many of us human beings who find themselves in that position. I sincerely hope that it has served this purpose adequately. The next chapter is brief, and ranges widely and speculatively, perhaps betraying the author's background in history, before switching to psychology in mid-life.

20 Conclusion and further implications

Summing up

This book is intended to inform and interest those who want to gain a better understanding of mental health breakdown, and, importantly, help those they encounter who are going through this experience. It contains enough detail of the therapy process to guide those in roles such as counsellors, coaches, etc. to be able to support someone who is struggling with their mental health the CCC way. The manual in Clarke & Nicholls (2018) would be a useful additional resource, and the two books essentially complement each other. However, it is hoped that the book will also be relevant for a much wider group of people who are confronted with the challenge of mental health breakdown in employees, supervisees, those in their care in their role as chaplains, study tutors, mentors and simply family and friends. It is argued that current, medicalized conceptualizations of mental health problems are unhelpful for the lay supporter and sufferer alike. They make abnormal the normality of human fallibility and in doing so over-complicate and stigmatize.

This book aims to strip away these complications, down to the bare realities of how human brains and emotions operate, and in so doing reveal our fundamental interdependence and potential for instability. This very instability, this picture of self as process and as shifting sands, offers hope for change and growth. By grasping the central role of mindful grounding, we can, at least fleetingly, take charge of the process. What this book does not offer is any certainty or guarantees. Life is an adventure, not a package holiday.

Throughout my career I have sought to increase recognition of the common humanity and common vulnerability that is inseparable from this approach. I have also pursued recognition of the centrality of relationship and the instability of the sense of self. An acceptance of uncertainty, and letting go of claims to certainty, is a recurring theme; one that is particularly relevant in the area of experience that steps beyond the threshold of shared reality; psychosis and the like. Mindful grounding in present, physical, reality, goes hand in hand with accepting and working with this threshold between shared and unshared reality (see Chapter 17), along with developing compassion for self and others, and for the different parts of the self; living and expressing emotions to positive effect, particularly the maligned emotion of anger. Hopefully this approach will be clear to those who have travelled the journey.

DOI: 10.4324/9781003081616-25

Further, CCC offers a new and challenging vision of the human being, founded in the ICS model of brain architecture, but reaching beyond the individual brain, and beyond the precisely knowable, into areas only touched by relationship and experience. This different vision of the human being and our place in the world has wider implications that I will attempt to sketch in for this concluding section.

Beyond the individual: the legacy of industrialization and colonialism

I have already mentioned that I am writing this in the midst of the COVID-19 pandemic, which has laid bare the fault lines of our society. The 'Black Lives Matter' movement has sprung into prominence at the same time, highlighting inequality and discrimination that have concerned me over decades. All this happens at a time when global heating and human degradation of the environment can no longer be ignored as it comes, literally, home to us, in terms of fire and flood, as well as destroying livelihoods in distant parts of the world. This in turn leads to pressure on resources, wars and migration to our shores.

Much of this book has concerned distorted patterns of relating and behaving, managed in ways that lead deeper into dysfunction. Because they are governed by emotion and hence the implicational, these reach beyond time and place. As mentioned in Chapter 6, the same processes can be observed within and between societies. Social ills, such as inequality, racism, austerity and the like, impact on the internal wellbeing; the felt sense, of individuals, and hence on their mental health. The resulting inability of individuals to achieve a satisfactory sense of self in turn leads to social ills such as addiction, crime, child abuse and domestic violence. A society infected in this way will in turn be more divided, less able to care for its members, more likely to turn on minorities and newcomers; more likely to turn on other societies, leading to the ultimate evil of warfare.

This captures only one dimension of the problem, the present time. We are talking about processes governed by the implicational, so operating outside of time. It is here we might find clues to some of the current distortions. Take the issue of racism. Those of us who benefit from the security and comfort of a Western lifestyle need to accept that the wealth on which this is founded entailed the appropriation of land occupied by less powerful (in terms of organization and weaponry) people, stealing their land and resources, and often involving slavery. Where more traditional societies were engulfed by a large influx of Western settlers, as in America and Australia, this led to systematic extermination of indigenous peoples, accompanied by cultural annihilation that assisted the process by demolishing their very identity.

This is a hard inheritance to acknowledge. Class divisions have similar, if less drastic, effects. Class divisions can often be traced to more distant conquest; castes in India and the Mogul invasions; the Norman aristocracy and the Anglo-Saxon plebs in England. Just as a therapy client might feel overwhelmed by the painful emotions at the heart of their diagram, and avoid or blot these out by some addictive behaviour, it is easy to feel helpless in the face of this burden foisted on us by our ancestors, from which we benefit, and choose to avoid or deny. Another factor is the natural anger towards those who make us feel bad, feel guilty. This can lead at best to estrangement between communities and, at worst, hostility. All these patterns can be seen in the relations between the races in Western societies. Relations between classes are not exempt either.

The environmental dimension

These processes do not just operate between people and peoples. The current predicament of our world points to the distorted relationship between people and planet. Hand in hand with the colonialism described above goes industrialization as the second plank of the runaway success of Western civilization. We have had the feast. We are now presented with the bill. Exploitation of resources, extermination of species, overwhelming of the environmental homeostasis with greenhouse gases and waste is now coming home in the form of melting ice-caps, wild fires and wild weather, and a host of other ills, making our home planet into an increasingly hostile environment. The COVID-19 pandemic, raging as I write this, is not a side issue, but a symptom of the unhealthy proximity between species and frantic global movement produced by our frenetic and over-crowded planet. It could be first of many.

So, our relationship with the planet, the environment, mirrors the destructive relationship between dominant and subordinated races outlined above. Our current level of comfort and control over the environment has been bought through ruthless exploitation, with no thought for the consequences, to the point where the earth's ability to sustain future generations of our species is now in question. As with relations between the races, a distorted relationship feels uncomfortable for the abuser as well as the abused. The main argument of this book demonstrates how unbearable feelings drive avoidance, denial and addictive behaviours.

CCC and this mess

Unsurprisingly, CCC does not offer a way out of this mess, but it does suggest possible approaches. In the same way as I emphasized that therapy is about healing the 'self-self' relationship, this is about recognizing that we are here dealing with relationships that have gone wrong, and working to heal them.

We obviously cannot change the past, so we need to accept and face it, however uncomfortable, and seek to heal our relationship with it and its chief victims. It is probably not possible at this stage to make truly meaningful reparation for the intercommunal past wrongs, and it could be argued that there is a limit to the extent to which the present generation should be held responsible for the actions of our forefathers. A wholehearted and humble acknowledgement that we are where we are, built on the injustices of the past, should go some way to creating a place from which we can go forward together. There is a balancing act to be accomplished here. If we (and here I am referring to the whole society, the dominant and subjugated) continue to ruminate on the ills of the past, we simply perpetuate rage and division.

We need to go forward together, in a way that does not perpetuate these divisions but seeks an inclusive and compassionate society, always aspiring to greater equality, so that we can actually meet the real challenges that face us without diverting energy into unproductive bitterness. Emotions can be employed to this end, in exactly the same way as for individual healing. We can mourn the sadness and loss of the lives that should have been, across the divides, together. Joanna Macey shows the way here in the field of environmental activism through 'the work that re-connects' (Macey & Brown 2014). The inevitable anger we need to redirect for justice work going forward.

Expressing and acting out compassion towards those suffering the effects of past wrongs is a start, meaning compassion towards our fellow beings on this planet, human and otherwise, and the planet itself. Compassion that truly opens ourselves to need is challenging, in the face of, for instance, mass migration. The anger that will keep us stuck if focused back towards the past, we can offer in the cause of justice; justice that is abundantly needed in the present and going forward. Justice leading to more equitable distribution of resources; justice that leads to putting the needs of the planet and future generations before comfort and convenience in the present. It is precisely the sensitive people; the people who have personally been wounded by life, who are capable of entering most deeply into these healing emotions – provided they have managed and been helped to free themselves from counterproductive coping strategies that otherwise keep them stuck and wounded, rendering the necessary energy unavailable.

As individuals, this sort of action can feel futile; a drop in the ocean, so that reaching out to like-minded others is the solution, and at this time, like-minded communities, bent on justice and compassion, are coming together. Extinction Rebellion and Black Lives Matter are examples here. For myself, the Spiritual Crisis Network UK seeks help and justice for those journeying, and perhaps getting lost, in the further reaches of the mind.

Central to the argument of this book is the theme of relationship; recognizing that these challenges are an issue of relationship; relationship between us and the planet; relationship between us and other species; relationship with all we hold dear and important. Could this help towards a corrective perspective on priorities? Acquisition, comfort, freedom to dash around, and enjoy a lifestyle we have become accustomed to pale into insignificance before what we are faced with. Stopping; mindfully taking in our surroundings; taking in the fullness of the essentials of our lives; just eating, drinking, sleeping, friendship, love; connecting with the beauty and welcome of our home the earth; reaching out to the wonder and the mystery of it all, the mystery of the unfathomable depths and breadths that lie 'beyond the threshold' in the transliminal – however we personally and our people choose to frame that. Perhaps that is a start? I am only a therapist. I do not know.

References

Ainsworth, M. D. S., Blehar, M., Waters, E. & Wall, S. (1978). *Patterns of Attachment.* Hillsdale, NJ: Erlbaum.

Araci, D. & Clarke, I. (2017): Investigating the efficacy of a whole team, psychologically informed, acute mental health service approach. *Journal of Mental Health,* 26, 307–311. http://dx.doi.org/10.3109/09638237.2016.1139065.

Bandura, A. (1969). *Behaviour Modification.* New York: Holt, Rinehart & Winston.

Bannister, D. & Fransella, F. (1971). *Inquiring Man.* Harmondsworth: Penguin.

Barnard, P. J. (2003). Asynchrony, implicational meaning and the experience of self in schizophrenia. In T. Kircher & A. David (Eds.), *The Self in Neuroscience and Psychiatry* (pp. 121–146). Cambridge: Cambridge University Press.

Barnard, P. J. (2010). Current developments in inferring cognitive capabilities from the archaeological traces left by stone tools: caught between a rock and a hard inference. In A. Nowell & I. Davidson (Eds.), *Stone Tools and the Evolution of Human Cognition* (pp. 207–226). Boulder, CO: University Press of Colorado.

Bateman, A. W. & Fonagy, P. (2004). *Psychotherapy for Borderline Personality Disorder: Mentalization Based Treatment.* Oxford: Oxford University Press.

Bebbington, P. E., Wilkins, S., Jones, P., Foerster, A., Murray, R. M., Toone, B. *et al.* (1993). Life events and psychosis: initial results from the Camberwell Collaborative Psychosis Study. *British Journal of Psychiatry,* 162, 358–362. http://bjp.rcpsych.org/content/162/1/72.full.pdf.

Beck, A. T. (1976). *Cognitive Therapy and Emotional Disorders.* New York: International Universities Press.

Bentall, R. P. (2003). *Madness Explained: Psychosis and Human Nature.* London: Allen Lane.

Bentall, R. P. (2009). *Doctoring the Mind: Why Psychiatric Treatments Fail.* London: Allen Lane.

Bomford, R. (1999). *The Symmetry of God.* London: Free Association Books.

Bowlby, J. (1969). *Attachment and Loss.* London: Basic Books.

Bowlby, J. (1988). *A Secure Base: Clinical Applications of Attachment Theory.* London: Basic Books.

Boyle, M. & Johnstone, L. (2014). Alternatives to psychiatric diagnosis. *Lancet Psychiatry,* 1, 409–411.

Boyle, M. (2002). *Schizophrenia: A Scientific Delusion?* London: Routledge.

Bracken, P., Thomas, P., Timimi, S., Asen, E., Behr, G., Beuster, C. *et al.* (2012). Psychiatry beyond the current paradigm. *The British Journal of Psychiatry,* 201, 430–434.

Brett, C., Heriot-Maitland, C., McGuire, P. & Peters, E. (2013). Predictors of distress associated with psychotic-like anomalous experiences in clinical and non-clinical populations. *British Journal of Clinical Psychology*, 11, 213–227.

Brett, C. M. C. (2010). Transformative crises. In I. Clarke (Ed.), *Psychosis and Spirituality: Consolidating the New Paradigm* (2nd Edition). Chichester: Wiley.

Brett, C. M. C., Johns, L., Peters, E. & McGuire, P. (2009). The role of metacognitive beliefs in determining the impact of anomalous experiences: a comparison of help-seeking and non-help-seeking groups of people experiencing psychotic-like anomalies. *Psychological Medicine*, 39, 939–950.

Brett, C. M. C., Peters, E. P., Johns, L. C., Tabraham, P., Valmaggia, L. R. & Mcguire, P. K. (2007). Appraisals of Anomalous Experiences Interview (AANEX): a multi-dimensional measure of psychological responses to anomalies associated with psychosis. *The British Journal of Psychiatry*, 191, 23–30.

Brewin, C. R. (2018). Memory and forgetting. *Current Psychiatry Reports*, 20 (10), 87. doi:10.1007/s11920-018-0950-7.

Brewin, C. R. (2011). The nature and significance of memory disturbance in posttraumatic stress disorder. *Annual Review Clinical Psychology*, 7, 203–227. doi:10.1146/annurev-clinpsy-032210-104544.

Brewin, C. R. (2001). A cognitive neuroscience account of posttraumatic stress disorder and its treatment. *Behaviour Research and Therapy*, 39, 373–393.

Brewin, C. R., Dalgleish, T. & Joseph, S. (1996). A dual representation theory of posttraumatic stress disorder. *Psychological Review*, 103, 670–686.

Brom, D., Kleber, R. J. & Defares, P. B. (1989). Brief psychotherapy for posttraumatic stress disorders. *Journal of Consulting and Clinical Psychology*, 57, 607–612.

Bullock, J., Whiteley, C., Moakes, K., Clarke, I. & Riches, S. (2020). Single-session Comprehend, Cope, and Connect intervention in acute and crisis psychology: a feasibility and acceptability study. *The Journal of Clinical Psychology and Psychotherapy*, 28, 219–225. doi:10.1002/cpp.2505.

Campbell, P., Dillon, J. & Longden, E. (2013). Service users and survivors. In J. Cromby, D. Harper & P. Reavey (Eds.) *Psychology, Mental Health and Distress* (pp. 139–157). Basingstoke: Palgrave Macmillan.

Carr, C. P., Martins, C. M. S, Stingle, A. M., Lemgruber V. B. & Juruena, M. F. (2013). The role of early life stress in adult psychiatric disorders: a systematic review according to childhood trauma subtypes. *Journal of Nervous and Mental Disease*, 201, 1007–1020.

Chabris, C. & Simons, D. (2010). *The Invisible Gorilla*. London: HarperCollins.

Chadwick P. K. (1992). *Borderline: A Psychological Study of Paranoia and Delusional Thinking*. London and New York: Routledge.

Claridge, G. S. (Ed.) (1997). *Schizotypy: Relations to Illness and Health*. Oxford: Oxford University Press.

Claridge, G. A. (2010). Spiritual experience: healthy psychoticism? In I. Clarke (Ed.), *Psychosis and Spirituality: Consolidating the New Paradigm* (2nd Edition). Chichester: Wiley.

Clarke, C. (2013). *Knowing, Doing and Being: New Foundations for Consciousness Studies*. Exeter: Imprint Academic.

Clarke, I. (2015). The Emotion Focused Formulation Approach: bridging individual and team formulation. *Clinical Psychology Forum*, 275, 28–32.

Clarke, I. (2013). Spirituality: a new way into understanding psychosis. In E. M. J. Morris, L. C. Johns & J. E. Oliver (Eds.), *Acceptance and Commitment Therapy and Mindfulness for Psychosis* (pp. 160–171). Chichester: Wiley-Blackwell.

Clarke, I. (Ed.) (2010a). *Psychosis and Spirituality: Consolidating the New Paradigm*. Chichester: Wiley.

Clarke, I. (2010b). 'What is real and what is not': towards a positive reconceptualisation of vulnerability to unusual experiences. In I. Clarke (Ed.), *Psychosis and Spirituality: Consolidating the New Paradigm* (2nd Edition) (pp. 195–204). Chichester: Wiley.

Clarke, I. (2010c). Psychosis and spirituality: the discontinuity model. In I. Clarke (Ed.), *Psychosis and Spirituality: Consolidating the New Paradigm* (2nd Edition) (pp. 101–114). Chichester: Wiley.

Clarke, I. (2008). *Madness, Mystery and the Survival of God*. Winchester: O Books.

Clarke, I. & Nicholls, H. (2018). *Third Wave CBT Integration for Individuals and Teams: Comprehend, Cope and Connect*. Abingdon: Routledge.

Clarke, I. & Wilson, H. (Eds.) (2008). *Cognitive Behaviour Therapy for Acute Inpatient Mental Health Units: Working with Clients, Staff and the Milieu*. London: Routledge.

Copeland, M. E. (1997). *Wellness Recovery Action Plan (WRAP)*. West Dummerton, VT: Peach Press.

Dana, D. (2018). *The Polyvagal Theory in Therapy: Engaging the Rhythm of Regulation*. London: Norton.

Decety, J. & Jackson, P. L. (2004). The functional architecture of human empathy. *Behavioural and Cognitive Neuroscience Reviews*, 3, 71–100.

Dennett, D. C. (1983). Artificial Intelligence and the strategies of psychological investigation. In J. Miller (Ed.), *States of Mind: Conversations with Psychological Investigators*. London: BBC.

Depue, R. A. & Morrone-Strupinsky, J. V. (2005). A neurobehavioural model of affiliative bonding. *Behavioural and Brain Sciences*, 28, 313–395.

Dillon, J. (2011). The personal is the political. In M. Rapley, J. Moncrieff & J. Dillon (Eds.), *De-Medicalizing Misery: Psychiatry, Psychology and the Human Condition* (pp. 141–157). London: Palgrave Macmillan.

Dillon, J. (2009). Jacqui Dillon. In M. Romme, S. Esche, J. Dillon *et al.* (Eds.) *Living With Voices: 50 Stories of Recovery* (pp. 188–193). Ross-on-Wye: PCCS Books.

Division of Clinical Psychology (2018). *Classification of Behaviour and Experience in Relation to Functional Psychiatric Diagnosis: Time for a Paradigm Shift*. Leicester: British Psychological Society.

Durrant, C., Clarke, I., Tolland, A. & Wilson, H. (2007). Designing a CBT service for an acute in-patient setting: a pilot evaluation study. *Clinical Psychology and Psychotherapy*, 14, 117–125.

Ehlers, A. & Clark, D. (2000). A cognitive model of posttraumatic stress disorder. *Behaviour Research & Therapy*, 38, 319–345.

Ellis, A. (1962). *Reason and Emotion in Psychotherapy*. New York: Lyle Stuart.

Eysenck, H. J. (1960). Personality and behaviour therapy. *Journal of the Royal Society of Medicine*, 53, 504–508.

Fox, M. (1983). *Original Blessing*. Santa Fe, NM: Bear & Co.

Gilbert, P. (2009). Evolved minds and compassion-focused imagery in depression. In L. Stopa (Ed.) *Imagery and the Threatened Self*. Abingdon: Routledge.

Gilbert, P. (Ed.) (2005). *Compassion: Conceptualisations, Research and Use in Psychotherapy*. London: Routledge.

Gilbert, P. (1992). *Depression: The Evolution of Powerlessness*. Hove, UK: Lawrence Erlbaum Associates.

Grey, N., Holmes, E. & Brewin, C. (2001). Peritraumatic emotional 'hotspots' in memory. *Behavioural and Cognitive Psychotherapy*, 29, 367–372.

Grof, C. & Grof, S. (1991). *The Stormy Search for the Self: Understanding and Living with Spiritual Emergency*. London: Mandala.

Haslam, C., Jetten, J., Cruwys, T., Dingle, G. & Haslam, S. A. (2018). *The New Psychology of Health: Unlocking the Social Cure*. Abingdon: Routledge.

Hayes, S., Strosahl, K. D. & Wilson, K. G. (1999). *Acceptance and Commitment Therapy*. New York: Guildford Press.

Hartley, J. (2010). Mapping our madness: the hero's journey as a therapeutic approach. In I. Clarke (Ed.), *Psychosis and Spirituality: Consolidating the New Paradigm* (2nd Edition) (pp. 227–239). Chichester: Wiley.

Heinz, A., Deserno, L. & Reininghaus, U. (2013). Urbanicity, social adversity and psychosis. *World Psychiatry*, 12 (3), 187–197.

Heriot-Maitland, C., Knight, M. & Peters, E. (2012). A qualitative comparison of psychotic-like phenomena in clinical and non-clinical populations. *British Journal of Clinical Psychology*, 51, 37–53. doi:10.1111/j.2044-8260.2011.02011.x.

Herman, J. (2001). *Trauma and Recovery* (2nd Edition). London: Pandora.

Jackson, M. C. (2010). The paradigm-shifting hypothesis: a common process in benign psychosis and psychotic disorder. In I. Clarke (Ed.), *Psychosis and Spirituality: Consolidating the New Paradigm* (2nd Edition) (pp. 139–153). Chichester: Wiley.

Jackson, M. C. (1997). Benign schizotypy? The case of spiritual experience. In G. S. Claridge (Ed.), *Schizotypy: Relations to Illness and Health*. Oxford: Oxford University Press.

James, W. (1902/1978). *The Varieties of Religious Experience*. New York: Longmans/The Modern Library.

Johnstone, L. (2014). *A Straight-talking Guide to Psychiatric Diagnosis*. Ross-on-Wye: PCCS Books.

Johnstone, L. & Boyle, M. with Cromby, J., Dillon, J., Harper, D., Kinderman, P., Longden, E., Pilgrim, D. & Read, J. (2018). *The Power Threat Meaning Framework: Towards the Identification of Patterns in Emotional Distress, Unusual Experiences and Troubled or Troubling Behaviour, as an Alternative to Functional Psychiatric Diagnosis*. Leicester: British Psychological Society. www.bps.org.uk/power-threat-meaning-framework.

Kabat-Zinn, J. (1996). *Full Catastrophe Living: Using the Wisdom of Your Body and Mind to Face Stress, Pain and Illness*. Bridgeton, NJ: Piatkus.

Kahneman, D. (2012). *Thinking Fast and Slow*. Harmondsworth: Penguin.

Kennedy, F., Kennerley, H. & Pearson, D. (Eds.) (2013). *Cognitive Behavioural Approaches to the Understanding and Treatment of Dissociation*. London: Routledge.

Kilpatrick, L. A. (2005). *Attachment, Evolution and the Psychology of Religion*. New York: Guildford Press.

Kinderman, P., Read, J., Moncrieff, J. *et al.* (2013). Drop the language of disorder. *Evidence-Based Mental Health*, 16 (1), 2–3.

Kirkbride, J. B., Jones, P. B., Ullrich, S. & Coid, J. W. (2012). Social deprivation, inequality, and the neighborhood-level incidence of psychotic syndromes in East London. *Schizophrenia Bulletin*, 151. http://schizophreniabulletin.oxfordjournals.org/content/40/1/169.full.pdf+html.

Laing R. D. (1965). *The Divided Self*. Harmondsworth: Penguin Books.

Laing, R. D. (1967). *The Politics of Experience*. Harmondsworth: Penguin.

Linehan, M. (1993). *Skills Training Manual for Treating Borderline Personality Disorder*. New York: Guildford Press.

Loewenthal, D. & Proctor, G. (Eds.) (2018). *Why Not CBT? Against and For CBT Revisited*. Monmouth: PCCS Books.

Longden, E. (2013). *Learning from the Voices in my Head.* New York: TED Conferences.

Longden, E., Madill, A. & Waterman, M. G. (2012). Dissociation, trauma and the role of the lived experience: toward a new conceptulization of voice hearing. *Psychological Bulletin,* 138 (1), 28–76.

Luck, S. J., Girelli, M., McDermott, M. T. & Ford, M. A. (1997). Bridging the gap between monkey neurophysiology and human perception: an ambiguity resolution theory of visual selective attention. *Cognitive Psychology,* 33, 64–87.

Macey, J. & Brown, M. Y. (2014). *Coming Back to Life: The Updated Guide to the Work that Reconnects.* Gabriola Island, BC: New Society Publishers.

McGilchrist, I. (2009). *The Master and his Emissary: The Divided Brain and the Making of the Western World.* New Haven & London: Yale University Press.

Martinez, A., Piff, P., Mendoza-Denton, R. *et al.* (2011). The power of a label: mental illness diagnoses, ascribed humanity and social rejection. *Journal of Social and Clinical Psychology,* 30, 1–23.

Masson, J. M. (1984). *The Assault on Truth: Freud's Suppression of the Seduction Theory.* New York: Farrar, Straus and Giroux.

Masson, J., Bernoussi, A., Cozette Mience, M. & Thomas, F. (2013). Complex trauma and Borderline Personality Disorder. *Open Journal of Psychiatry,* 3, 403–407. http://dx.doi.org/10.4236/ojpsych.2013.34044.

Mattick, R. P. & Peters, L. (1988). Treatment of severe social phobia: effects of guided exposure with and without cognitive restructuring. *Journal of Consulting and Clinical Psychology,* 56, 251–260.

Moncrieff, J. (2010). Psychiatric diagnosis as a political device. *Social Theory & Health,* 8, 370–382.

Moncrieff, J. (2008). *The Myth of the Chemical Cure: A Critique of Psychiatric Drug Treatment.* Basingstoke: Palgrave Macmillan.

Morkved, N., Endsjo, M., Winje, D., Johnsen, E., Dovran, A., Arefjord, K., Kroken, R. A., Helle, S., Anda-Agotnes, L. G., Rettenbacher, M. A., Huber, N. & Loberg, E. M. (2017). Childhood trauma in schizophrenia spectrum disorder as compared to other mental health disorders. *Psychosis,* 9, 48–56.

Murray, S. O., Kersten, D., Olshausen, B. A., Schrater, P. & Woods, D. L. (2002). Shape perception reduces activity in human primary visual cortex. *Proceedings of the National Academy of Sciences of the United States,* 99 (23) 15164–15169, https://doi.org/10.1073/pnas.192579399.

Naeem, F., Habib, N., Gul, M. & Khalid, M. (2016). A qualitative study to explore patients', carers' and health professionals' views to culturally adapt CBT for psychosis (CBTp) in Pakistan. *Behavioural & Cognitive Psychotherapy,* 44, 43–55.

Naeem, F., Phiri, P., Munshi, T., Rathod, S., Ayub, M., Gobbi, M. & Kingdon, D. (2015). Using cognitive behaviour therapy with South Asian Muslims: Findings from the culturally sensitive CBT project. *International Review of Psychiatry,* 27, 233–246.

National Institute for Health and Clinical Excellence (2009). *Borderline Personality Disorder: Treatment and Management.* London: NICE.

NIMHE (2003). *Personality Disorder: No Longer a Diagnosis of Exclusion.* London: Department of Health.

Otto, R. (1917/1958). *The Idea of the Holy: An Inquiry into the non-Rational Factor in the Idea of the Divine and its Relation to the Rational* (trans. J.W. Harvey). London: Oxford University Press.

Owen, M., Sellwood, W., Kan, S., Murray, J. & Sarsam, M. (2015). Group CBT for psychosis: a longitudinal, controlled trial with inpatients. *Behaviour Research and Therapy* 65, 76–85.

Paterson, C., Karatzias, T., Dickson, A., Harper, S., Dougall, N. & Hutton, P. (2018). Psychological therapy for inpatients receiving acute mental health care: A systematic review and meta-analysis of controlled trials. *British Journal of Clinical Psychology*, 57, 453–472. doi:10.1111/bjc.12182.

Peters, E. R. (2010). Are delusions on a continuum? The case of religious and delusional beliefs. In I. Clarke (Ed.), *Psychosis and Spirituality: Consolidating the New Paradigm* (2nd Edition). Chichester: Wiley.

Peters, E. R., Day, S., McKenna, J. & Orbach, G. (1999). The incidence of delusional ideation in religious and psychotic populations. *British Journal of Clinical Psychology*, 38, 83–96.

Pilgrim, D. (2015). *Understanding Mental Health: A Critical Realist Exploration*. London: Routledge.

Porges, S. W. (2009). The polyvagal theory: new insights into adaptive reactions of the autonomic nervous system. *Cleveland Clinical Journal of Medicine*, 76 (2), S86–S90.

The Power Threat Meaning Framework (2019). www.bps.org.uk/power-threat-meaning-framework.

Radin, D. (2006). *Entangled Minds*. New York: Paraview.

Razzaque, R. & Wood, L. (2015). Open dialogue and its relevance to the NHS: opinions of NHS staff and service users. *Community Mental Health Journal*. doi:10.1007/s10597-015-9849-5.

Read, J. (2007). Why promulgating biological ideology increases prejudice against people labelled 'schizophrenic'. *Australian Psychologist*, 42, 118–128.

Read, J. & Bentall, R. P. (2012). Negative childhood experiences and mental health: theoretical, clinical and primary prevention implications. *British Journal of Psychiatry*, 200, 89–91.

Read, J., Bentall, R. P. & Fosse, R. (2009). Time to abandon the bio-bio-bio model of psychosis: exploring the epigenetic and psychological mechanisms by which adverse life events lead to psychotic symptoms. *Epidemiol Psychiatric Society*, 18, 299–310.

Read, J., Haslam, N. & Magliano, L. (2013). Prejudice, stigma and 'schizophrenia': the role of bio-genetic ideology. In J. Read & J. Dillon (Eds.), *Models of Madness: Psychological, Social and Biological Approaches to Psychosis* (2nd Edition) (pp.157–177). London: Routledge.

Read, J., Os, J., Morrison, A. P. & Ross, C. A. (2005). Childhood trauma, psychosis and schizophrenia: a literature review with theoretical and clinical implications. *Acta Psychiatrica Scandinavica*, 112, 330–350.

Rogers, C. (1961). *On Becoming a Person: A Therapist's View of Psychotherapy*. London: Constable.

Rogers, C. (1951). *Client-Centered Therapy*. New York: Houghton Mifflin.

Rosenfield, S. (2012). Triple jeopardy? Mental health at the intersection of gender, race, and class. *Social Science & Medicine*, 74 (1), 1791–1796.

Romme, M. & Escher, S. (1989). *Accepting Voices*. London: Mind Publications.

Rowan, J. (1990). *Subpersonalities: The People Inside Us*. London: Routledge.

Ryle, A. & Kerr, I. B. (2004). *Introducing Cognitive Analytic Therapy*. Chichester: Wiley.

Schore, A. N. (1994). *Affect Regulation and the Origin of the Self: The Neurobiology of Emotional Development*. Hillsdale, NJ: Lawrence Erlbaum Associates.

Segal, Z. W., Williams, J. M. G. & Teasdale, J. D. (2002). *Mindfulness-Based Cognitive Therapy for Depression: A New Approach to Preventing Relapse*. New York: Guilford Press.

Seikkula, J., Aaltonen, J., Alakare, B., Haarakangas, K., Keranen, J. & Lehtinen, K. (2006). Five year experience of first episode non-affective psychosis in open-dialogue approach: Treatment principles, follow-up outcomes, and two case studies. *Psychotherapy Research*, 16 (02), 214–228.

Shapiro, F. & Maxfield, L. (2002). Eye movement desensitization and reprocessing (EMDR): Information processing in the treatment of trauma. *Journal of Clinical Psychology*, 58, 933–946.

Shepherd, G., Boardman, J. & Slade, M. (2012). *Making Recovery a Reality*. London: Sainsbury Centre.

Skinner, B. F. (1974). *About Behaviourism*. London: Jonathan Cape.

Stone, H. & Stone, S. (1993). *Embracing Our Selves: The Voice Dialogue Training Manual*. California: Nataraj Publishing.

Svanholmer, E. & May, R. (2018). Ideas on how to talk supportively with voices. Openmindedonline.com. https://openmindedonline.com/2018/10/14/talking-with-voices-article-and-video.

Sweeney, A., Clement, S., Filson, B. & Kennedy, A. (2016). Trauma-informed mental healthcare in the UK: what is it and how can we further its development? *Mental Health Review Journal*, 21, 174–192.

Szasz, T. S. (1974). *The Myth of Mental Illness*. New York: Harper and Row.

Teasdale, J. D. & Barnard, P. J. (1993). *Affect, Cognition and Change: Remodelling Depressive Thought*. Hove: Lawrence Erlbaum Associates.

Thalbourne, M. A. & Delin, P. S. (1994). A common thread underlying belief in the paranormal, creative personality, mystical experience, and psychopathology. *Journal of Parapsychology*, 58, 3–38.

Tobert, N. (2017). *Cultural Perspectives on Mental Wellbeing: Spiritual Interpretations of Symptoms in Medical Practice*. London: Jessica Kingsley.

Tobert, N. (2014). *Spiritual Psychiatries: Mental Health Practices in India and UK*. London: Aethos.

van der Kolk, B. (2014). *The Body Keeps the Score: Brain, Mind, and Body in the Healing of Trauma*. New York: Viking.

Varese, F., Smeets, F., Drukker, M., Lieverse, R., Lataster, T., Viechtbauer, W. & Bentall, R. P. (2012). Childhood adversities increase the risk of psychosis: a meta-analysis of patient-control, prospective and cross-sectional cohort studies. *Schizophrenia Bulletin*, 38, 661–671.

Walsch, N. D. (1995). *Conversations with God: An Uncommon Dialogue*. London: Hodder & Stoughton.

Warner, R. (2007). Review of recovery from schizophrenia: an international perspective. a report from the WHO Collaborative Project, the International Study of Schizophrenia. *American Journal of Psychiatry*, 164, 1444–1445.

Warner, R. (2004). *Recovery from Schizophrenia: Psychiatry and Political Economy*. Hove: Psychology Press.

Whitaker, R. (2010). *Anatomy of an Epidemic*. New York: Broadway Paperbacks.

Williams, J. M. G., Barnhofer, T., Crane, C., Hermans, D., Raes, F., Watkins, E. & Dalgleish, T. (2007). Autobiographical memory specificity and emotional disorder. *Psychological Bulletin*, 133, 122–148. doi:10.1037/0033-2909.133.1.122.

Wilson, J. P. & Thomas, R. B. (2004). *Empathy in the Treatment of Trauma and PTSD*. London: Routledge.

Index

Page numbers in *italics* refer to figures.

174   *Index*

For Product Safety Concerns and Information please contact our EU
representative GPSR@taylorandfrancis.com Taylor & Francis Verlag GmbH,
Kaufingerstraße 24, 80331 München, Germany

Printed and bound by CPI Group (UK) Ltd, Croydon, CR0 4YY

08/06/2025

01897002-0020